Eng.d by H.B.Hall, from the original Painting by Stuart.

KEY-NOTES

OF

AMERICAN LIBERTY;

COMPRISING

THE MOST IMPORTANT SPEECHES, PROCLAMATIONS, AND ACTS OF CONGRESS, FROM THE FOUNDATION OF THE GOVERNMENT TO THE PRESENT TIME.

WITH A

HISTORY OF THE FLAG,

BY A DISTINGUISHED HISTORIAN.

Illustrated.

NEW YORK:
E. B. TREAT & CO.
654 BROADWAY.

CHICAGO, ILLINOIS: R. C. TREAT AND C. W. LILLEY.
B. C. BAKER, DETROIT, MICH. I. C. BRAINARD, ST. LOUIS, MO.
A. O. BRIGGS, CLEVELAND, O. M. PITMAN & CO., BOSTON, MASS.
A. L. TALCOTT, PITTSBURG, PA.

MACDONALD & STONE, PRINTERS AND STEREOTYPERS, 48 CENTRE STREET, N. Y.

PREFACE.

THIS book appeals to the patriotic sentiments of all classes of readers. In its pages will be found those words of burning eloquence which lighted the fires of the American Revolution, stirring the hearts of our fathers to do battle for our independence; the words of wisdom which brought our ship of state safely through the storms of strife into the calms of peace, and all of the most important speeches and proclamations of our statesmen which guided our country during critical periods of our political life. It is a book of our country as a whole; all must read it with emotions of gratitude and pride at the grandeur and stability of our institutions as exemplified by the eloquent words of the statesmen and leading spirits of the great Republic.

First in its pages, appropriately, will be found the "Declaration of Independence," the great corner stone of American liberty; and as a fitting close, one of our most distinguished historians has furnished a "History of the Flag,"—the Flag of the Union, the sacred emblem around which are clustered the memories of the thousands of heroes who have struggled to sustain it untarnished against both foreign and domestic foes. To the Declaration of Independence, Constitution of the United States, and Washington's Farewell Address—truly "Key Notes to American Liberty"—have been added many important proclamations and congressional acts of a later day, namely: President Jackson's famous Nullification Proclamation to South Carolina, The Monroe Doctrine, Dred Scott Decision, Neutrality laws, with numerous documents, state papers and statistical matter growing out of the late Rebellion; all of which will be read with new and ever increasing interest. And as long as our Republic endures, these pages will be cherished as the representative of all that is great and good in our country; and will prove incentives to our children to follow in the footsteps of the patriots by whose genius and valor our institutions have been cherished and preserved, and liberty, like water made to run throughout the land free to all.

CONTENTS.

Key-Notes of American Liberty.

DECLARATION OF INDEPENDENCE.

In Congress, July 4, 1776.

By the Representatives of the United States, in Congress assembled.

A DECLARATION.

When, in the course of human events, it becomes necessary for one people to dissolve the political bands which have connected them with another, and to assume among the powers of the earth the separate and equal station to which the laws of nature and of nature's God entitle them, a decent respect for the opinions of mankind requires that they should declare the causes which impel them to the separation.

We hold these truths to be self-evident:—that all men are created equal; that they are endowed by their Creator with certain inalienable rights; that among these are life, liberty, and the pursuit of happiness; that to secure these rights, governments are instituted among men, deriving their just powers from the consent of the governed; that whenever any form of government becomes destructive of these ends it is the right of the people to alter or to abolish it, and to institute a new government, laying its foundation on such principles, and organizing its powers in such form, as to them shall seem most likely to effect their safety and happiness. Prudence, indeed, will dictate that governments long established should not be changed for light and transient causes; and accordingly all experience hath shown that mankind are more disposed to suffer, while evils are sufferable, than to right themselves by abolishing the forms to which they are accustomed. But when a long train of abuses and usurpations, pursuing invariably the same object, evinces a design to reduce them under absolute despotism, it is their right, it is their duty, to throw off such government, and to provide new guards for their future security. Such has been the patient sufferance of these colonies; and such is now the necessity which constrains them to alter their former system of government. The history of the present King of Great Britain is a history of repeated injuries and usurpations, all having in direct object the establishment of an absolute tyranny over these States. To prove this, let facts be submitted to a candid world.

He has refused his assent to laws the most wholesome and necessary for the public good.

He has forbidden his governors to pass laws of immediate and pressing importance, unless suspended in their operation till his assent should be obtained; and, when so suspended, he has utterly neglected to attend to them.

He has refused to pass other laws for the accommodation of large districts of people, unless those people would relinquish the right of representation in the legislature—a right inestimable to them, and formidable to tyrants only.

He has called together legislative bodies at places unusual, uncomfortable, and distant from the depository of their public records, for the sole purpose of fatiguing them into compliance with his measures.

He has dissolved representative houses repeatedly, for opposing, with manly firmness, his invasions on the right of the people.

He has refused, for a long time after such dissolutions, to cause others to be elected; whereby the legislative powers, incapable of annihilation, have returned to the people at large for their exercise; the State remaining, in the mean time, exposed to all the danger of invasion from without and convulsions within.

He has endeavored to prevent the population of these States; for that purpose obstructing the laws for naturalization of foreigners, refusing to pass others to encourage their migration hither, and raising the conditions of new appropriations of lands.

He has obstructed the administration of justice, by refusing his assent to laws for establishing judiciary powers.

He has made judges dependent on his will alone for the tenure of their offices and the amount and payment of their salaries.

He has erected a multitude of new offices, and sent hither swarms of officers, to harrass our people and eat out their substance.

He has kept among us, in times of peace, standing armies, without the consent of our legislatures.

He has affected to render the military independent of and superior to the civil power.

He has combined with others to subject us to a jurisdiction foreign to our constitution and unacknowledged by our laws; giving his assent to their acts of pretended legislation,—

For quartering large bodies of armed troops among us:

For protecting them, by a mock trial, from punishment for any murders which they should commit on the inhabitants of these States:

For cutting off our trade with all parts of the world:

For imposing taxes on us without our consent:

For depriving us, in many cases, of the benefits of trial by jury:

For transporting us beyond seas, to be tried for pretended offences:

For abolishing the free system of English law in a neighboring province, establishing therein an arbitrary government, and enlarging its boundaries so as to render it at once an example and fit instrument for introducing the same absolute rule into these colonies:

For taking away our charters, abolishing our most valuable laws, and altering fundamentally the forms of our government:

For suspending our own legislatures, and declaring themselves invested with power to legislate for us in all cases whatsoever.

He has abdicated government here by declaring us out of his protection, and waging war against us

He has plundered our seas, ravaged our coasts,

burned our towns, and destroyed the lives of our people.

He is at this time transporting large armies of foreign mercenaries, to complete the works of death, desolation, and tyranny, already begun, with circumstances of cruelty and perfidy scarcely paralleled in the most barbarous ages, and totally unworthy the head of a civilized nation.

He has constrained our fellow-citizens, taken captive on the high seas, to bear arms against their country, to become the executioners of their friends and brethren, or to fall themselves by their hands.

He has excited domestic insurrections amongst us, and has endeavored to bring on the inhabitants of our frontiers the merciless Indian savages, whose known rule of warfare is an undistinguished destruction of all ages, sexes, and conditions.

In every stage of these oppressions we have petitioned for redress in the most humble terms; our petitions have been answered only by repeated injury. A prince whose character is thus marked by every act which may define a tyrant, is unfit to be the ruler of a free people.

Nor have we been wanting in attention to our British brethren. We have warned them, from time to time, of attempts made by their legislature to extend an unwarrantable jurisdiction over us. We have reminded them of the circumstances of our emigration and settlement here. We have appealed to their native justice and magnanimity, and we have conjured them, by the ties of our common kindred, to disavow these usurpations, which would inevitably interrupt our connections and correspondence. They, too, have been deaf to the voice of justice and consanguinity. We must therefore acquiesce in the necessity which denounces our separation, and hold them, as we hold the rest of mankind, enemies in war—in peace, friends.

We, therefore, the representatives of the United States of America, in General Congress assembled, appealing to the Supreme Judge of the world for the rectitude of our intentions, do, in the name and by the authority of the good people of these colonies, solemnly publish and declare that these United Colonies are, and of good right ought to be, free and independent States; that they are absolved from all allegiance to the British crown, and that all political connection between them and the State of Great Britain is, and ought to be, totally dissolved; and that, as free and independent States, they have full power to levy war, conclude peace, contract alliances, establish commerce, and to do all other acts and things which independent States may of right do. And for the support of this declaration, with a firm reliance on the protection of Divine Providence, we mutually pledge to each other our lives, our fortunes, and our sacred honor.

Signed by order and in behalf of the Congress.

JOHN HANCOCK, *President.*

Attested, CHARLES THOMPSON, *Secretary.*

NEW HAMPSHIRE.

Josiah Bartlett,
William Whipple,
Matthew Thornton.

MASSACHUSETTS BAY.

Samuel Adams,
John Adams,
Robert Treat Paine,
Eldridge Gerry.

RHODE ISLAND, ETC.

Stephen Hopkins,
William Ellery.

CONNECTICUT.

Roger Sherman,
Samuel Huntington,
William Williams,
Oliver Wolcott.

NEW YORK.

William Floyd,
Philip Livingston,
Francis Lewis,
Lewis Morris.

NEW JERSEY.

Richard Stockton,
John Witherspoon,
Francis Hopkinson,
John Hart,
Abraham Clark.

PENNSYLVANIA.

Robert Morris,
Benjamin Rush,
Benjamin Franklin,
John Morton,
George Clymer,
James Smith,
George Taylor,
James Wilson,
George Ross.

DELAWARE.

Cæsar Rodney,
George Read,
Thomas M'Kean.

MARYLAND.

Samuel Chase,
William Paca,
Thomas Stone,
Charles Carroll, of Carrollton.

VIRGINIA.

George Wythe,
Richard Henry Lee,
Thomas Jefferson,
Benjamin Harrison,
Thomas Nelson, jr.,
Francis Lightfoot Lee,
Carter Braxton.

NORTH CAROLINA.

William Hooper,
Joseph Hewes,
John Penn.

SOUTH CAROLINA.

Edward Rutledge,
Thomas Heyward, jr.,
Thomas Lynch, jr.,
Arthur Middleton.

GEORGIA.

Button Gwinnett,
Lyman Hall,
George Walton.

CONSTITUTION OF THE UNITED STATES.

WE, the People of the United States, in order to form a more perfect union, establish justice, insure domestic tranquillity, provide for the common defence, promote the general welfare, and secure the blessings of liberty to ourselves and our posterity, do ordain and establish this Constitution for the United States of America.

ARTICLE I.

§ I.—All legislative powers herein granted shall be vested in a Congress of the United States, which shall consist of a Senate and House of Representatives.

§ II.—1. The House of Representatives shall be composed of members chosen every second year by the people of the several States; and the electors in each State shall have the qualifications requisite for electors of the most numerous branch of the State legislature.

2. No person shall be a representative who shall not have attained the age of twenty-five years, and been seven years a citizen of the United States, and who shall not, when elected, be an inhabitant of the State in which he shall be chosen.

3. Representatives and direct taxes shall be apportioned among the several States which may be included within this Union, according to their respective numbers, which shall be determined by adding to the whole number of free persons, including those bound to service for a term of years, and excluding Indians not taxed, three-fifths of all other persons. The actual enumeration shall be made within three years after the first meeting of the Congress of the United States, and within every subsequent term of ten years, in such manner as they shall by law direct. The number of representatives shall not exceed one for every thirty thousand, but each State shall have at least one representative; and until such enumeration shall be made, the State of *New Hampshire* shall be entitled to choose three; *Massachusetts*, eight; *Rhode Island and Providence Plantations*, one; *Connecticut*, five; *New York*, six; *New Jersey*, four; *Pennsylvania*, eight; *Delaware*, one; *Maryland*, six; *Virginia*, ten; *North Carolina*, five; *South Carolina*, five; *Georgia*, three.

4. When vacancies happen in the representation

of any State, the executive authority thereof shall issue writs of election to fill such vacancies.

5. The House of Representatives shall choose their speaker and other officers, and shall have the sole power of impeachment.

§ III.—1. The Senate of the United States shall be composed of two senators from each State, chosen by the legislature thereof, for six years; and each senator shall have one vote.

2. Immediately after they shall be assembled in consequence of the first election, they shall be divided, as equally as may be, into three classes. The seats of the senators of the first class shall be vacated at the expiration of the second year, of the second class at the expiration of the fourth year, and the third class at the expiration of the sixth year, so that one third may be chosen every second year; and if vacancies happen, by resignation or otherwise, during the recess of the legislature of any State, the executive thereof may make temporary appointments until the next meeting of the legislature, which shall then fill such vacancies.

3. No person shall be a Senator who shall not have attained the age of thirty years, and been nine years a citizen of the United States, and who shall not, when elected, be an inhabitant of that State for which he shall be chosen.

4. The Vice-President of the United States shall be President of the Senate, but shall have no vote, unless they be equally divided.

5. The Senate shall choose their other officers, and also a president pro tempore in the absence of the Vice-President, or when he shall exercise the office of President of the United States.

6. The Senate shall have the sole power to try all impeachments. When sitting for that purpose, they shall be on oath or affirmation. When the President of the United States is tried, the chief justice shall preside; and no person shall be convicted without the concurrence of two-thirds of the members present.

7. Judgment, in cases of impeachment, shall not extend further than to removal from office, and disqualification to hold and enjoy any office of honor, trust, or profit under the United States; but the party convicted shall, nevertheless, be liable and subject to indictment, trial, judgment, and punishment, according to law.

§ IV.—1. The times, places, and manner of holding elections for Senators and representatives shall be prescribed in each State by the legislature thereof; but the Congress may, at any time, by law, make or alter such regulations, except as to the places of choosing senators.

2. The Congress shall assemble at least once in every year; and such meeting shall be on the first Monday in December, unless they shall by law appoint a different day.

§ V.—1. Each house shall be judge of the elections, returns, and qualifications of its own members; and a majority of each shall constitute a quorum to do business; but a smaller number may adjourn from day to day, and may be authorized to compel the attendance of absent members, in such manner and under such penalties as each house may provide.

2. Each house may determine the rules of its proceedings, punish its members for disorderly behavior, and, with the concurrence of two-thirds, expel a member.

3. Each house shall keep a journal of its proceedings, and from time to time publish the same, excepting such parts as may, in their judgment, require secrecy; and the yeas and nays of the members of either house on any question shall, at the desire of one-fifth of those present, be entered on the journal.

4. Neither house, during the session of Congress, shall, without the consent of the other, adjourn for more than three days, nor to any other place than that in which the two houses shall be sitting.

§ VI.—1. The senators and representatives shall

receive a compensation for their services, to be ascertained by law, and paid out of the treasury of the United States. They shall, in all cases except treason, felony, and breach of the peace, be privileged from arrest during their attendance at the session of their respective houses, and in going to or returning from the same; and for any speech or debate in either house they shall not be questioned in any other place.

2. No senator or representative shall, during the time for which he was elected, be appointed to any civil office under the authority of the United States which shall have been created, or the emoluments whereof shall have been increased, during such time; and no person holding any office under the United States shall be a member of either house during his continuance in office.

§ VII.—1. All bills for raising revenue shall originate in the House of Representatives; but the Senate may propose or concur with amendments, as on other bills.

2. Every bill which shall have passed the House of Representatives and the Senate shall, before it becomes a law, be presented to the President of the United States; if he approve, he shall sign it; but if not, he shall return it with his objections, to that house in which it shall have originated, who shall

enter the objections at large on their journal, and proceed to reconsider it. If, after such reconsideraation, two thirds of that house shall agree to pass the bill, it shall be sent, together with the objections, to the other house; and if approved by two-thirds of that house it shall become a law. But in all such cases the votes of both houses shall be determined by yeas and nays; and the name of the persons voting for and against the bill shall be entered on the journals of each house respectively. If any bill shall not be returned by the President within ten days (Sundays excepted) after it shall have been presented to him, the same shall be a law, in like manner as if he had signed it, unless Congress, by their adjournment, prevent its return; in which case it shall not be a law.

3. Every order, resolution, or vote to which the concurrence of the Senate and House of Representatives may be necessary (except on a question of adjournment) shall be presented to the President of the United States, and before the same shall take effect shall be approved by him, or, being disapproved by him, shall be repassed by two-thirds of the Senate and House of Representatives, according to the rules and limitations prescribed in the case of a bill.

§ VIII.—The Congress shall have power—

1. To lay and collect taxes, duties, imposts, and excises; to pay the debts and provide for the common defence and general welfare of the United States; but all duties, imposts, and excises shall be uniform throughout the United States:

2. To borrow money on the credit of the United States:

3. To regulate commerce with foreign nations, and among the several States, and with the Indian tribes:

4. To establish a uniform rule of naturalization, and uniform laws on the subject of bankruptcies, throughout the United States:

5. To coin money, regulate the value thereof, and of foreign coin, and fix the standard of weights and measures:

6. To provide for the punishment of counterfeiting the securities and current coin of the United States:

7. To establish post offices and post roads:

8. To promote the progress of science and useful arts, by securing, for limited times, to authors and inventors the exclusive right to their respective writings and discoveries:

9. To constitute tribunals inferior to the Supreme Court:

10. To define and punish piracies and felonies

committed on the high seas, and offences against the law of nations:

11. To declare war, grant letters of marque and reprisal, and make rules concerning captures on land and water:

12. To raise and support armies; but no appropriation of money to that use shall be for a longer term than two years:

13. To provide and maintain a navy:

14. To make rules for the government and regulation of the land and naval forces:

15. To provide for calling forth the militia to execute the laws of the Union, suppress insurrections, and repel invasions

16. To provide for organizing, arming, and disciplining the militia, and for governing such part of them as may be employed in the service of the United States, reserving to the States respectively the appointment of the officers, and the authority of training the militia, according to the discipline prescribed by Congress:

17. To exercise exclusive legislation, in all cases whatsoever, over such district (not exceeding ten miles square) as may, by cession of particular States, and the acceptance of Congress, become the seat of government of the United States, and to exercise like authority over all places purchased by the consent of

the legislature of the State in which the same shall be, for the erection of forts, magazines, arsenals, dock yards, and other needful building: And,

18. To make all laws which shall be necessary and proper for carrying into execution the foregoing powers, and all other powers vested by this Constitution in the government of the United States, or in any department or officer thereof.

§ IX.—1. The migration or importation of such persons as any of the States, now existing, shall think proper to admit, shall not be prohibited by the Congress prior to the year one thousand eight hundred and eight; but a tax or duty may be imposed on such importation, not exceeding ten dollars for each person.

2. The privilege of the writ of habeas corpus shall not be suspended, unless when, in cases of rebellion or invasion, the public safety may require it.

3. No bill of attainder, or ex post facto law, shall be passed.

4. No capitation or other direct tax shall be laid, unless in proportion to the census or enumeration herein before directed to be taken.

5. No tax or duty shall be laid on articles exported from any States. No preference shall be given, by any regulation of commerce or revenue, to the ports of one State over those of another; nor

shall vessels bound to or from one State be obliged to enter, clear, or pay duties in another.

6. No money shall be drawn from the treasury but in consequence of appropriations made by law; and a regular statement and account of the receipts and expenditurss of all public money shall be published from time to time.

7. No title of nobility shall be granted by the United States; and no person holding any office of profit or trust under them shall, without the consent of the Congress, accept of any present, emolument, office, or title of any kind whatever, from any king, prince, or foreign State.

§ X.—1. No state shall enter into any treaty, alliance, or confederation; grant letters of marque and reprisal; coin money; emit bills of credit; make any thing but gold and silver coin a tender in payment of debts; pass any bill of attainder, ex post facto law, or impairing the obligation of contracts; or grant any title of nobility.

2. No State shall, without the consent of Congress, lay any imposts or duties on imports or exports, except what may be absolutely necessary for executing its inspection laws; and the net produce of all duties and imposts laid by any State on imports or exports shall be for the use of the treasury of the United States; and all such laws shall be

subject to the revision and control of the Congress. No State shall, without the consent of Congress, lay any duty on tonnage, keep troops or ships of war in time of peace, enter into any agreement or compact with another State or with a foreign power, or engage in war, unless actually invaded, or in such imminent danger as will not admit of delay.

ARTICLE II.

§ I.—1. The executive power shall be vested in a President of the United States of America. He shall hold his office during the term of four years, and, together with the Vice-President, chosen for the same term, be elected as follows:

2. Each State shall appoint, in such manner as the legislature thereof may direct, a number of electors, equal to the whole number of senators and representatives to which the State may be entitled in the Congress; but no senator or representative, or person holding an office of trust or profit under the United States, shall be appointed an elector.

3. [Annulled. See Amendments, Art. 12.]

4. The Congress may determine the time of choosing the electors, and the day on which they shall give their votes, which day shall be the same throughout the United States.

5. No person except a natural-born citizen, or a citizen of the United States at the time of the adoption of this Constitution, shall be eligible to the office of President; neither shall any person be eligible to that office who shall not have attained the age of thirty-five years, and been fourteen years a resident within the United States.

6. In case of the removal of the President from office, or of his death, resignation, or inability to discharge the powers and duties of said office, the same shall devolve on the Vice-President; and the Congress may by law provide for the case of removal, death, resignation, or inability both of the President and Vice-President, declaring what officer shall then act as President, and such officer shall act accordingly, until the disability be removed, or a President shall be elected.

7. The President shall, at stated times, receive for his services a compensation which shall neither be increased nor diminished during the period for which he shall have been elected; and he shall not receive, within that period, any other emolument from the United States, or any of them.

8. Before he enter on the execution of his office, he shall take the following oath or affirmation:—

"I do solemnly swear (or affirm) that I will faithfully execute the office of President of the

United States, and will, to the best of my ability, preserve, protect, and defend the Constitution of the United States."

§ II.—1. The President shall be commander-in-chief of the army and navy of the United States, and of the militia of the several States, when called into the actual service of the United States: he may require the opinion, in writing, of the principal officer in each of the executive departments upon any subject relating to the duties of their respective offices; and he shall have power to grant reprieves and pardons for offences against the United States, except in cases of impeachment.

2. He shall have power, by and with the advice and consent of the Senate, to make treaties, provided two-thirds of the Senators present concur; and he shall nominate, and by and with the advice and consent of the Senate shall appoint, ambassadors, other public ministers, and consuls, judges of the Supreme Court, and all other officers of the United States whose appointments are not herein otherwise provided for, and which shall be established by law. But the Congress may, by law, vest the appointment of such inferior officers as they think proper in the President alone, in the courts of law, or in the heads of departments.

3. The President shall have power to fill up all

vacancies that may happen during the recess of the Senate, by granting commissions, which shall expire at the end of the next session.

§ III.—He shall, from time to time, give to the Congress information of the state of the Union, and recommend to their consideration such measures as he shall judge necessary and expedient; he may, on extraordinary occasions, convene both houses, or either of them, and in case of disagreement between them with respect to the time of adjournment, he may adjourn them to such time as he shall think proper; he shall receive ambassadors and other public ministers; he shall take care that the laws are faithfully executed; and shall commission all the officers of the United States.

§ IV.—The President, Vice-President, and all civil officers of the United States, shall be removed from office on impeachment for, and conviction of, treason, bribery, or other high crimes and misdemeanors.

ARTICLE III.

§ I.—The judicial power of the United States shall be vested in one Supreme Court, and in such inferior courts as the Congress may, from time to time, ordain and establish. The judges, both of the Supreme and inferior courts, shall hold their offices during good behavior, and shall, at stated times, receive for their services a compensation which shall not be diminished during their continuance in office.

§ II.—1. The judicial power shall extend to all cases in law and equity arising under this Constitution, the laws of the United States, and treaties made, or which shall be made under their authority; to all cases affecting ambassadors, and other public ministers, and consuls; to all cases of admiralty and maritime jurisdiction; to controversies to which the United States shall be a party; to controversies between two or more States; between a State and citizens of another State; between citizens of different States; between citizens of the same State, claiming lands under grants of different States, and between a State, or the citizens thereof, and foreign States, citizens, or subjects.

2. In all cases affecting ambassadors, other public ministers, and consuls, and those in which a State shall be a party, the Supreme Court shall have original jurisdiction. In all other cases before mentioned, the Supreme Court shall have appellate jurisdiction, both as to law and fact, with such exceptions, and under such regulations, as the Congress shall make.

3. The trial of all crimes, except in cases of impeachment, shall be by jury; and such trial shall be

held in the State where such crimes shall have been committed; but when not committed within any State, the trial shall be at such place or places as the Congress may by law have directed.

§ III.—1. Treason against the United States shall consist only in levying war against them, or in adhering to their enemies, giving them aid and comfort. No person shall be convicted of treason, unless on the testimony of two witnesses to the same overt act, or confessions in open court.

2. The Congress shall have power to declare the punishment of treason; but no attainder of treason shall work corruption of blood, or forfeiture, except during the life of the person attainted.

ARTICLE IV.

§ I.—Full faith and credit shall be given in each State to the public acts, records, and judicial proceedings of every other State. And the Congress may, by general laws, prescribe the manner in which such acts, records, and proceedings shall be proved, and the effect thereof.

§ II.—1. The citizens of each State shall be entitled to all privileges and immunities of citizens in the several States.

2. A person charged in any State with treason,

felony, or other crime, who shall flee from justice, and be found in another State, shall, on demand of the executive authority of the State from which he fled, be delivered up to be removed to the State having jurisdiction of the crime.

3. No person held to service or labor in one State, under the laws thereof, escaping into another, shall, in consequence of any law or regulation therein, be discharged from such service or labor, but shall be delivered up on claim of the party to whom such service or labor may be due.

§ III.—1. New States may be admitted by the Congress into this Union; but no new State shall shall be formed or erected within the jurisdiction of any other State; nor any State be formed by the junction of two or more States, or parts of States, without the consent of the legislature of the States concerned, as well as of the Congress.

2. The Congress shall have power to dispose of and make all needful rules and regulations respecting the territory or other property belonging to the United States; and nothing in this Constitution shall be so construed as to prejudice any claims of the United States, or of any particular State.

§ IV.—The United States shall guaranty to every State of this Union a republican form of government, and shall protect each of them against invasion, and, on application of the legislature, or of the executive, (when the legislature cannot be convened,) against domestic violence.

ARTICLE V.

The Congress, whenever two-thirds of both houses shall deem it necessary, shall propose amendments to this Constitution, or, on the application of the legislatures of two-thirds of the several States, shall call a convention for proposing amendments, which, in either case, shall be valid to all intents and purposes, as part of this Constitution, when ratified by the legislatures of three-fourths of the several States, or by conventions in three-fourths thereof, as the one or the other mode of ratification may be proposed by the Congress; provided that no amendment which may be made prior to the year one thousand eight hundred and eight shall in any manner affect the first and fourth clauses in the ninth section of the first article; and that no State, without its consent, shall be deprived of its equal suffrage in the Senate.

ARTICLE VI.

1. All debts contracted, and engagements entered into, before the adoption of this Constitution, shall be as valid against the United States under this Constitution as under the confederation.

2. This Constitution, and the laws of the United States which shall be made in pursuance thereof, and all treaties made, or which shall be made, under the authority of the United States, shall be the supreme law of the land; and the judges in every State shall be bound thereby; any thing in the Constitution or laws of any State to the contrary notwithstanding.

3. The senators and representatives before mentioned, and the members of the several State legislatures, and all executive and all judicial officers, both of the United States and of the several States, shall be bound by oath or affirmation to support this Constitution; but no religious test shall ever be required as a qualification to any office or public trust under the United States.

ARTICLE VII.

The ratification of the conventions of nine States shall be sufficient for the establishment of this Constitution between the States so ratifying the same.

Done in Convention, by the unanimous consent of the States present, the seventeenth day of September, in the year of our Lord one thousand seven hundred and eighty-seven, and of the Independence of the United States of America the twelfth. In witness whereof, we have hereunto subscribed our names.

GEORGE WASHINGTON,
President, and Deputy from Virginia.

NEW HAMPSHIRE.

John Langdon,
Nicholas Gilman.

MASSACHUSETTS.

Nathaniel Gorham,
Rufus King.

CONNECTICUT.

Wm. Samuel Johnson,
Roger Sherman.

NEW YORK.

Alexander Hamilton.

NEW JERSEY.

William Livingston,
David Brearley,
William Patterson,
Jonathan Dayton.

PENNSYLVANIA.

Benjamin Franklin,
Thomas Mifflin,
Robert Morris,
George Clymer,
Thomas Fitzsimons,
Jared Ingersoll,
James Wilson,
Gouverneur Morris.

DELAWARE.

George Read,
Gunning Bedford, jr.,
John Dickinson,
Richard Bassett,
Jacob Broom.

MARYLAND.

James McHenry,
Daniel of St. Tho. Jenifer,
Daniel Carroll.

VIRGINIA.

John Blair,
James Madison, jr.

NORTH CAROLINA.

William Blount,
Rich. Dobbs Spaight,
Hugh Williamson.

SOUTH CAROLINA.

John Rutledge,
Charles C. Pinckney,
Charles Pinckney,
Pierce Butler.

GEORGIA.

William Few,
Abraham Baldwin.

Attest, WILLIAM JACKSON, *Secretary.*

AMENDMENTS TO THE CONSTITUTION.

Art. I.—Congress shall make no law respecting an establishment of religion, or prohibiting the free exercise thereof; or abridging the freedom of speech, or of the press; or the right of the people peaceably to assemble and to petition the government for a redress of grievances.

Art. II.—A well-regulated militia being necessary to the security of a free State, the right of the people to keep and bear arms shall not be infringed.

Art. III.—No soldier shall, in time of peace, be quartered in any house without the consent of the owner, nor in time of war but in a manner to be prescribed by law.

Art. IV.—The right of the people to be secure in their persons, houses, papers, and effects, against unreasonable searches and seizures, shall not be violated; and no warrants shall issue but upon probable cause, supported by oath or affirmation, and particularly describing the place to be searched, and the persons or things to be seized.

ART. V.—No person shall be held to answer for a capital or otherwise infamous crime, unless on a presentment or indictment of a grand jury, except in cases arising in the land or naval forces, or in the militia when in actual service, in time of war or public danger; nor shall any person be subject for the same offence to be twice put in jeopardy of life or limb; nor shall be compelled, in any criminal case, to be witness against himself, nor be deprived of life, liberty, or property, without due process of law; nor shall private property be taken for public use without just compensation.

ART. VI.—In all criminal prosecutions, the accused shall enjoy the right to a speedy and public trial by an impartial jury of the State and district wherein the crime shall have been committed, which district shall have been previously ascertained by law, and to be informed of the nature and cause of the accusation; to be confronted with the witnesses against him; to have compulsory process for obtaining witnesses in his favor; and to have the assistance of counsel for his defence.

ART. VII.—In suits of common law, where the value in controversy shall exceed twenty dollars, the right of trial by jury shall be preserved; and no fact, tried by a jury, shall be otherwise reexamined in any court of the United States than according to the rules of the common law.

ART. VIII.—Excessive bail shall not be required, nor excessive fines imposed, nor cruel and unusual punishments inflicted.

ART. IX.—The enumeration in the Constitution of certain rights shall not be construed to deny or disparage others retained by the people.

ART. X.—The powers not delegated to the United States by the Constitution, nor prohibited by it to the States, are reserved to the States respectively, or to the people.

ART. XI.—The judicial power of the United States shall not be construed to extend to any suit in law or equity commenced or prosecuted against one of the United States by citizens of another State, or by citizens or subjects of any foreign State.

ART. XII.—The electors shall meet in their respective States, and vote by ballot for President and Vice-President, one of whom, at least, shall not be an inhabitant of the same State with themselves; they shall name in their ballots the person voted for as President, and in distinct ballots the person voted for as Vice-President; and they shall make distinct lists of all persons voted for as President, and of all persons voted for as Vice-President, and of the number of votes for each; which lists they shall sign and certify, and transmit, sealed, to the seat of government of the United States, directed to the president of the Senate. The president of the Senate shall, in the presence of the Senate and House of Representatives, open all the certificates, and the votes shall then be counted; the person having the greatest number of votes for President shall be President, if such number be a majority of the whole number of electors appointed; and if no person have such a majority, then from the persons having the highest number, not exceeding three, on the list of those voted for as President, the House of Represen tatives shall choose immediately, by ballot, the President. But, in choosing the President, the votes shall be taken by States, the representation from each State having one vote; a quorum for this purpose shall consist of a member or members from two thirds of the States, and a majority of all the States shall be necessary to a choice. And if the House of Representatives shall not choose a President, whenever the right of choice shall devolve upon them, before the fourth day of March next following, then the Vice-President shall act as President, as in the case of the death or other constitutional disability of the President.

2. The person having the greatest number of votes as Vice-President shall be the Vice-President, if such number be a majority of the whole number of electors appointed; and if no person have a majority, then from the two highest numbers on the list the Senate shall choose the Vice-President; a quorum for the purpose shall consist of two-thirds of the whole number of senators, and a majority of the whole number shall be necessary to a choice.

3. But no person constitutionally ineligible to the office of President shall be eligible to that of Vice-President of the United States.

THE CONSTITUTIONAL AMENDMENT.

ARTICLE V. of the Constitution of the United States clearly and distinctly sets forth the mode and manner in which that instrument may be amended, as follows:

"The Congress, whenever two-thirds of both Houses shall deem it necessary, shall propose amendments to this Constitution, or, on the application of the Legislatures of two-thirds of the several States, shall call a convention for proposing amendments, which in either case shall be valid to all intents and purposes, as part of this Constitution, when ratified by the Legislatures of three-fourths of the several States, or by conventions in three-fourths thereof, as the one or the other mode of ratification may be proposed by the Congress."

In accordance with this article of the Constitution, the following resolution was proposed in the Senate, on February 1, 1864, adopted April 8, 1864, by a vote of 38 to 6, and was proposed in the House June 15, 1864, adopted Jan. 31, 1865, by a vote of 119 to 56:

Resolved, By the Senate and House of Representatives of the United States of America, in Congress assembled, two-thirds of both Houses concurring, that the following article be proposed to the Legislatures, of the several States, as an amendment to the constitution of the United States, which, when ratified by three-fourths of said Legislatures, shall be valid to all intents and purposes, as apart of the said Constitution, namely:

Art. XIII. 1st. Neither slavery nor involuntary servitude, except as a punishment for crime, whereof the party shall have been duly convicted, shall exist within the United States, or any place subject to their jurisdiction.

The amendment was now sent by the Secretary of State to the Governors of the several States for ratification by the Legislatures; a majority vote in three-fourths being required to make it a law of the land.

On Dec. 18, 1865, Secretary Seward officially announced to the country the ratification of the Amendment as follows:

To all to whom these presents may come, Greeting:

Know ye, That, whereas the Congress of the United States, on the 1st of February last, passed a resolution, which is in the words following, namely:

"A resolution submitting to the Legislatures of the several States a proposition to amend the Constitution of the United States."

"*Resolved*, By the Senate and House of Representatives of the United States of America in Congress assembled, two-thirds of both Houses concurring, that the following article be proposed to the Legislatures of the several States as an Amendment to the Constitution of the United States, which, when ratified by three-fourths of said Legislatures, shall be valid to all intents and purposes as a part of said Constitution, namely:

"'ARTICLE XIII.

"'SECTION 1. Neither slavery nor involuntary servitude, except as a punishment for crime, whereof the party shall have been duly convicted, shall exist within the United States, or any place subject to their jurisdiction.

"'SECTION 2. Congress shall have power to enforce this article by appropriate legislation.'"

And whereas, It appears from official documents on file in this Department, that the Amendment to the Constitution of the United States proposed as aforesaid, has been ratified by the Legislatures of the States of Illinois, Rhode Island, Michigan, Maryland, New York, West Virginia, Maine, Kansas, Massachusetts, Pennsylvania, Virginia, Ohio, Missouri, Nevada, Indiana, Louisiana, Minnesota, Wisconsin, Vermont, Tennessee, Arkansas, Connecticut, New Hampshire, South Carolina, Alabama, North Carolina, and Georgia, in all 27 States.

And whereas, The whole number of States in the United States is 36.

And whereas, The before specially named States, whose Legislatures have ratified the said proposed Amendment, constitute three-fourths of the whole number of States in the United States:

Now, therefore, be it known that I, William H. Seward, Secretary of State of the United States, by virtue and in pursuance of the second section of the act of Congress, approved the 20th of April, 1818, entitled "An act to provide for the publication of the laws of the United States, and for other purposes," do hereby certify that the Amendment aforesaid has become valid to all intents and purposes as a part of the Constitution of the United States.

In testimony whereof, I have hereunto set my hand and caused the seal of the Department of State to be affixed.

Done at the City of Washington, this 18th day of December, in the year of our Lord 1865, and of the Independence of the United States of America the 90th.

WM. H. SEWARD, *Secretary of State.*

PROPOSED AMENDMENTS.

ADOPTED BY CONGRESS JUNE 13TH, 1866, AND WHEN RATIFIED BY TWO-THIRDS OF THE LEGISLATURES BECOMES A PART OF THE CONSTITUTION.

THE joint resolution as passed is as follows:

Resolved, By the Senate and House of Representatives of the United States of America, in Congress assembled, (two-thirds of both Houses concurring), That the following article be proposed to the Legislatures of the several States, as an amendment to the Constitution of the United States, which, when ratified by three-fourths of said Legislatures, shall be valid as part of the Constitution, namely:

ARTICLE —.

§ 1. All persons born or naturalized in the United States, and subject to the jurisdiction thereof, are citizens of the United States and the States wherein they reside. No State shall make or enforce any law which shall abridge the privileges or immunities of citizens of the United States; nor shall any State deprive any person of life, liberty or happiness, without due process of law, nor deny to any person within its jurisdiction the equal protection of the laws.

§ 2. Representatives shall be apportioned among the several States according to their respective numbers, counting the whole number of persons, excluding Indians not taxed. But whenever the right to vote at any election for the choice of electors for President and Vice-President, representatives in Congress, executive and judicial officers, or members of the Legislature thereof, is denied to any of the male inhabitants of such State, being 21 years of age, and citizens of the United States, or in any way abridged, except for participation in rebellion or other crime, the basis of representation therein shall be reduced in the proportion which the number of such male citizens shall bear to the whole number of male citizens 21 years of age in such State.

§ 3. That no person shall be a Senator or Representative in Congress, or elector of President and Vice President, or hold any office, civil or military, under the United States, or under any State, who, having previously taken an oath as a member of Congress, or as an officer of the United States, or as a member of any State Legislature, or as an executive or judicial officer of any State, to support the Constitution of the United States, shall have engaged in insurrection or rebellion against the same, or given aid and comfort to the enemies thereof. But Congress may, by a vote of two-thirds of each House, remove such disabilities.

§ 4. The validity of the public debt of the United States authorized by law, including debts incurred for payment of pensions and bounties for services in suppressing insurrection or rebellion, shall not be questioned. But neither the United States or any State shall assume or pay any debt or obligation incurred in aid of insurrection or rebellion against the United States, or any claim for the loss or emancipation of any slave; but all such debts, obligations, and claims shall be held illegal and void.

§ 5. The Congress shall have power to enforce, by appropriate legislation, the provisions of this article.

THE ORDINANCE OF 1787.

Passed by Congress previous to the Adoption of the New Constitution, and subsequently adopted by Congress, Aug. 7, 1789, *entitled, "An Ordinance for the Government of the Territory of the United States north-west of the River Ohio."*

(All the Articles of this ordinance, previous to Article VI., relate to the organization and powers of the government of the territory, the following section being all that relates to slavery.)

ARTICLE VI.

There shall be neither slavery nor involuntary servitude in the said territory, otherwise than in punishment of crimes, whereof the party shall have been duly convicted: Provided always, that any person escaping into the same, from whom labor or service is lawfully claimed in any one of the original States, such fugitive may be lawfully reclaimed and conveyed to the person claiming his or her labor or service, as aforesaid.

Done by the United States in Congress assembled the thirteenth day of July, in the year of our Lord 1787, and of the sovereignty and Independence the twelfth.

WILLIAM GRAYSON, *Chairman.*

CHARLES THOMPSON, *Secretary.*

THE FUGITIVE SLAVE BILL OF 1793.

ADOPTED FEBRUARY 12, 1793.

An Act respecting Fugitives from Justice, and Persons escaping from the Service of their Masters.

Be it enacted by the Senate and House of Representatives of the United States of America in Congress assembled, That whenever the executive authority of any State in the Union, or of either of the territories north-west or south of the River Ohio, shall demand any person, as a fugitive from justice, of the executive authority of any such State or Territory to which such person shall have fled, and shall, moreover, produce the copy of an indictment found, or an affidavit made before a magistrate of any State or Territory as aforesaid, charging the person so demanded with having committed treason, felony, or other crime, certified as authentic by the governor or chief magistrate of the State or Territory from whence the person so charged fled, it shall be the duty of the executive authority of the State or Territory to which such person shall have fled, to cause him or her to be arrested and secured, and notice of the arrest to be given to the executive authority making such demand, or to the agent of such authority appointed to receive the fugitive, and to cause the fugitive to be delivered to such agent when he shall appear. But if no such agent shall appear within six months from the time of the arrest, the prisoner may be discharged. And all costs or expenses incurred in the apprehending, securing, and transmitting such fugitive to the State or Territory making such demand, shall be paid by such State or Territory.

And be it further enacted, That any agent appointed as aforesaid, who shall receive the fugitive into his custody, shall be empowered to transport him or her to the State or Territory from which he or she shall have fled. And if any person or persons shall by force set at liberty or rescue the fugitive from such agent while transporting as aforesaid, the person or persons so offending shall, on conviction, be fined not exceeding five hundred dollars, and be imprisoned not exceeding one year.

And be it also enacted, That when a person held

to labor in any of the United States, or in either of the Territories on the north-west or south of the River Ohio, under the laws thereof, shall escape into any other of the said States or Territory, the person to whom such labor or service may be due, his agent or attorney, is hereby empowered to seize or arrest such fugitive from labor, and to take him or her before any judge of the Circuit or District Courts of the United States, residing or being within the State, or before any magistrate of a county, city, or town corporate, wherein such seizure or arrest shall be made, and upon proof to the satisfaction of such judge or magistrate, either by oral testimony or affidavit taken before, and certified by, a magistrate of any such State or Territory, that the person so seized or arrested doth, under the laws of the State or Territory from which he or she fled, owe services or labor to the person claiming him or her, it shall be the duty of such judge or magistrate to give a certificate thereof to such claimant, his agent or attorney, which shall be sufficient warrant for removing the said fugitive from labor to the State or Territory from which he or she fled.

And be it further enacted, That any person who shall knowingly and willingly obstruct or hinder such claimant, his agent or attorney, in so seizing or arresting such fugitive from labor, or shall rescue such fugitive from such claimant, his agent or attorney, when so arrested pursuant to the authority herein given or declared, or shall harbor or conceal such person after notice that he or she was a fugitive from labor as aforesaid, shall, for either of the said offences, forfeit and pay the sum of five hundred dollars. Which penalty may be recovered by and for the benefit of such claimant, by action of debt, in any court proper to try the same; saving, moreover, to the person claiming such labor or service, his right of action for or on account of the said injuries, or either of them.

THE FUGITIVE SLAVE BILL OF 1850.

SIGNED SEPTEMBER 18, 1850.

An Act to amend, and supplementary to the Act entitled "An Act respecting Fugitives from Justice, and Persons escaping from the Service of their Masters," approved February twelfth, one thousand seven hundred and ninety-three.

Be it enacted by the Senate and House of Representatives of the United States of America in Congress assembled, That the persons who have been, or may hereafter be, appointed commissioners, in virtue of any act of Congress, by the Circuit Courts of the United States, and who, in consequence of such appointment, are authorized to exercise the powers that any justice of the peace, or other magistrate of any of the United States, may exercise in respect to offenders for any crime or offence against the United States, by arresting, imprisoning, or bailing the same under and by virtue of the thirty-third section of the act of the twenty-fourth of September, seventeen hundred and eighty-nine, entitled "An Act to establish the judicial courts of the United States," shall be, and are hereby, authorized and required to exercise and discharge all the powers and duties conferred by this act.

And be it further enacted, That the Superior Court of each organized Territory of the United States shall have the same power to appoint commissioners to take acknowledgments of bail and affidavits, and to take depositions of witnesses in civil causes, which is now possessed by the Circuit Court of the United States; and all commissioners who shall hereafter be appointed for such purposes by the Supreme Court of any organized Territory of the United States, shall possess all the powers, and exercise all the duties, conferred by law upon the commissioners appointed by the Circuit Courts of the United States for similar purposes, and shall moreover exercise and discharge all the powers and duties conferred by this act.

And be it further enacted, That the Circuit Courts of the United States, and the Superior Courts of each organized Territory of the United States, shall from time to time enlarge the number of commissioners, with a view to afford reasonable facilities to reclaim fugitives from labor, and to the prompt discharge of the duties imposed by this act.

And be it further enacted, That the commissioners above named shall have concurrent jurisdiction with the judges of the Circuit and District Courts of the United States, in their respective circuits and districts within the several States, and the judges of the Superior Courts of the Territories severally and collectively, in term time and vacation; and shall grant certificates to such claimants upon satisfactory proof being made, with authority to take and remove such fugitives from service or labor, under the restrictions herein contained, to the State or Territory from which such persons may have escaped or fled.

And be it further enacted, That it shall be the duty of all marshals and deputy marshals to obey and execute all warrants and precepts issued under the provisions of this act, when to them directed; and should any marshal or deputy marshal refuse to receive such warrant, or other process, when tendered, or to use all proper means diligently to execute the same, he shall, on conviction thereof, be fined in the sum of one thousand dollars, to the use of such claimant, on the motion of such claimant, by the Circuit or District Court for the district of such marshal; and after arrest of such fugitive, by such marshal or his deputy, or whilst at any time in his custody, under the provisions of this act, should such fugitive escape, whether with or without the assent of such marshal or his deputy, such marshal shall be liable, on his official bond, to be prosecuted for the benefit of such claimant, for the full value of the service or labor of said fugitive in the State, Territory, or district whence he escaped; and the better to enable said commissioners, when thus appointed, to execute their duties faithfully and efficiently, in conformity with the requirements of the constitution of the United States, and of this act, they are hereby authorized and empowered, within their counties respectively, to appoint, in writing under their hands, any one or more suitable persons, from time to time, to execute all such warrants and other process as may be issued by them in the lawful performance of their respective duties; with authority to such commissioners, or the persons to be appointed by them, to execute process as aforesaid, to summon and call to their aid the bystanders, or *posse comitatus* of the proper county, when necessary to insure a faithful observance of the clause of the constitution referred to, in conformity with the provisions of this act; and all good citizens are hereby commanded to aid and assist in the prompt and efficient execution of this law, whenever their services may be required, as aforesaid, for that purpose; and said warrants shall run, and be executed by said officers, any where in the State within which they are issued.

And be it further enacted, That when a person held to service or labor in any State or Territory of the United States has heretofore or shall hereafter escape into another State or Territory of the United States, the person or persons to whom such service or labor may be due, or his, her, or their agent or attorney, duly authorized by power of attorney, in writing acknowledged and certified under the seal of some legal officer or court of the State or Territory in which the same may be executed, may pursue and reclaim such fugitive person, either by procuring a warrant from some one of the courts, judges, or commissioners aforesaid, of the proper circuit, district, or county, for the apprehension of such fugitive from service or labor, or by seizing and arresting such fugitive where the same can be done without process, and by taking, or causing such person to be taken forthwith before such court, judge, or commissioner, whose duty it shall be to hear and determine the case of such claimant in a summary manner; and upon satisfactory proof being made, by deposition or affidavit, in writing, to be taken and certified by such court, judge, or commissioner, or by other satisfactory testimony, duly taken and certified by some court, magistrate, justice of the peace, or other legal officer authorized to administer an oath and take depositions under the laws of the State or Territory from which such person owing service or labor may have escaped, with a certificate of such magistracy, or other authority as aforesaid, with the seal of the proper court or officer thereto attached, which seal shall be sufficient to establish the competency of the proof, also by affidavit, of the identity of the person whose service or labor is claimed to be due as aforesaid, that the person so arrested does in fact owe service or labor to the person or persons claiming him or her, in the State or Territory from which such fugitive may have escaped as aforesaid, and that said person escaped, to make out and deliver to such claimant, his or her agent or attorney, a certificate setting forth the substantial facts as to the service or labor due from such fugitive to the claimant, and of his or her escape from the State or

Territory in which such service or labor was due to the State or Territory in which he or she was arrested, with authority to such claimant, or his or her agent or attorney, to use such reasonable force and restraint as may be necessary, under the circumstances of the case, to take and remove such fugitive person back to the State or Territory whence he or she may have escaped as aforesaid. In no trial or hearing under this act shall the testimony of such alleged fugitive be admitted in evidence; and the certificates in this and the first (fourth) section mentioned, shall be conclusive of the right of the person or persons in whose favor granted, to remove such fugitive to the State or Territory from which he escaped, and shall prevent all molestation of such person or persons by any process issued by any court, judge, magistrate, or other person whomsoever.

And be it further enacted, That any person who shall knowingly and willingly obstruct, hinder, or prevent such claimant, his agent or attorney, or any person or persons lawfully assisting him, her, or them, from arresting such a fugitive from service or labor, either with or without process as aforesaid, or shall rescue or attempt to rescue such fugitive from service or labor from the custody of such claimant, his or her agent or attorney, or other person or persons lawfully assisting as aforesaid, when so arrested pursuant to the authority herein given and declared, or shall aid, abet, or assist such person so owing service or labor as aforesaid, directly or indirectly, to escape from such claimant, his agent or attorney, or other person or persons legally authorized as aforesaid, or shall harbor or conceal such fugitive, so as to prevent the discovery and arrest of such person, after notice or knowledge of the fact that such person was a fugitive from service or labor as aforesaid, shall, for either of said offences, be subject to a fine not exceeding one thousand dollars, and imprisonment not exceeding six months, by indictment and conviction before the District Court of the United States for the district in which such offence may have been committed, or before the proper court of criminal jurisdiction, if committed within any one of the organized Territories of the United States, and shall moreover forfeit and pay, by way of civil damages to the party injured by such illegal conduct, the sum of one thousand dollars for each fugitive so lost as aforesaid, to be recovered by action of debt in any of the district or territorial courts aforesaid, within whose jurisdiction the said offence may have been committed.

And be it further enacted, That the marshals, their deputies, and the clerks of the said district and territorial courts, shall be paid for their services the like fees as may be allowed to them for similar services in other cases; and where such services are rendered exclusively in the arrest, custody, and delivery of the fugitive to the claimant, his or her agent or attorney, or where such supposed fugitive may be discharged out of custody for the want of sufficient proof as aforesaid, then such fees are to be paid in the whole by such claimant, his agent or attorney; and in all cases where the proceedings are before a commissioner, he shall be entitled to a fee of ten dollars in full for his services in each case, upon the delivery of the said certificate to the claimant, his or her agent or attorney; or a fee of five dollars in cases where the proof shall not, in the opinion of such commissioner, warrant such certificate and delivery, inclusive of all services incident to such arrest or examination, to be paid in either case by the claimant, his or her agent or attorney. The person or persons authorized to execute the process to be issued by such commissioner for the arrest and detention of fugitives from service or labor as aforesaid, shall also be entitled to a fee of five dollars each, for each person he or they may arrest and take before any such commissioner, as aforesaid, at the instance and request of such claimant, with such other fees as may be deemed reasonable by such commissioners for such other additional services as may be necessarily performed by him or them ; such as attending at the examination, keeping the fugitive in custody, and providing him with food and lodging during his detention and until the final determination of such commissioner; and, in general, for performing such other duties as may be required by such claimant, his or her attorney or agent, or commissioner in the premises. Such fees to be made up in conformity with the fees usually charged by the officers of the courts of juctice within the proper district or county, as near as may be practicable, and paid by such claimants, their agents or attorneys, whether such supposed fugitives from service or labor be ordered to be delivered to such claimants by the final determination of such commissioner or not.

And be it further enacted, That, upon affidavit made by the claimant of such fugitive, his agent or attorney, after such certificate has been issued that he has reason to apprehend that such fugitive will be rescued by force from his or her possession before he can be taken beyond the limits of the State in which the arrest is made, it shall be the duty of the officer making the arrest to retain such fugitive in his custody, and to remove him to the State whence he fled, and there deliver him to said claimant, his agent or attorney. And to this end, the officer aforesaid is hereby authorized and required to employ so many persons as he may deem necessary to overcome such force, and to retain them in his service so long as circumstances may require. The said officer and his assistants while so employed to receive the compensation, and to be allowed the same expenses, as are now allowed by law for transportation of criminals, to be certified by the judge of the district within which the arrest is made, and paid out of the Treasury of the United States.

And be it further enacted, That when any person held to service or labor in any State or Territory, or in the District of Columbia, shall escape therefrom, the party to whom such service or labor may be due, his, her, or their agent or attorney, may apply to any court of record therein, or judge thereof in vacation, and make satisfactory proof to such court, or judge in vacation, of the escape aforesaid, and that the person escaping owed service or labor to such party. Whereupon the court shall cause a record to be made of the matters so proved, and also a general description of the person so escaping with such convenient certainty as may be; and a transcript of such record, authenticated by the attestation of the clerk and of the seal of the said court, being produced in any other State, Territory, or district in which the person so escaping may be found, and being exhibited to any judge, commissioner, or other officer authorized by the law of the United States to cause persons escaping from service or labor to be delivered up, shall be held and taken to be full and conclusive evidence of the fact of the escape, and that the service or labor of the person escaping is due to the party in such record mentioned. And upon the production by the said party of other and further evidence if necessary, either oral or by affidavit, in addition to what is contained in the said record of the identity of the person escaping, he or she shall be delivered up to the claimant. And the said court, commissioner, judge, or other person authorized by this act to grant certificates to claimants of fugitives, shall, upon the production of the record and other evidences aforesaid, grant to such claimant a certificate of his right to take any such person identified and proved to be owing service or labor as aforesaid, which shall authorize such claimant to seize or arrest and transport such person to the State or Territory from which he escaped. *Provided*, That nothing herein contained shall be construed as requiring the production of a transcript of such record as evidence as aforesaid. But in its absence the claim shall be heard and determined upon other satisfactory proofs, competent in law.

THE MISSOURI COMPROMISE.

ADOPTED MARCH 6, 1820.

An Act to authorize the People of the Missouri Territory to form a Constitution and State Government, and for the Admission of such State into the Union on an equal Footing with the original States, and to prohibit Slavery in certain Territories.

(All the previous sections of this act relate entirely to the formation of the Missouri Territory in the usual form of territorial bills, the 8th section only relating to the slavery question.)

And be it further enacted, That in all that Territory ceded by France to the United States, under the name of Louisiana, which lies north of thirty-six degrees and thirty minutes north latitude, not included within the limits of the State contemplated by their act, slavery and involuntary servitude, otherwise than in the punishment of crimes, whereof the parties shall have been duly convicted, shall be, and is hereby, forever prohibited. *Provided always*, That any person escaping into the same, from whom labor or service is lawfully claimed, in any State or Territory of the United States, such fugitive may be lawfully reclaimed and conveyed to the person claiming his or her labor or service as aforesaid.

THE STATES OF THE UNION.

The following is a list of the States constituting the Union, with the dates of their admission. The thirty-six stars in our national flag are therefore designated as under:

Delaware	Dec. 7, 1787.	Indiana	Dec. 11, 1816.
Pennsylvania	Dec. 12, 1787.	Mississippi	Dec. 16, 1817.
New Jersey	Dec. 13, 1787.	Illinois	Dec. 3, 1818.
Georgia	Jan. 2, 1788.	Alabama	Dec. 14, 1819.
Connecticut	Jan. 9, 1788.	Maine	March 15, 1820.
Massachusetts	Feb. 6, 1788.	Missouri	Aug. 10, 1821.
Maryland	April 28, 1788.	Arkansas	June 15, 1836.
South Carolina	May 23, 1788.	Michigan	Jan. 26, 1837.
N. Hampshire	June 21, 1788.	Florida	March 3, 1845.
Virginia	June 26, 1788.	Texas	Dec. 29, 1845.
New York	July 26, 1788.	Iowa	Dec. 28, 1846.
N. Carolina	Nov. 21, 1789.	Wisconsin	May 29, 1848.
Rhode Island	May 29, 1790.	California	Sept. 9, 1850.
Vermont	March 4, 1791.	Minnesota	Dec., 1857.
Kentucky	June 1, 1792.	Oregon	Dec., 1858.
Tennessee	June 1, 1796.	Kansas	March, 1862.
Ohio	Nov. 29, 1802.	West Virginia	Feb. 1863.
Louisiana	April 8, 1812.	Nevada	Oct., 1864.

INAUGURAL ADDRESS OF GEORGE WASHINGTON.

FIRST PRESIDENT OF THE UNITED STATES, DELIVERED APRIL 30, 1789.

Fellow-Citizens of the Senate and House of Representatives—Among the vicissitudes incident to life, no event could have filled me with greater anxieties than that of which the notification was transmitted by your order, and received on the fourteenth day of the present month. On the one hand I was summoned by my country, whose voice I can never hear but with veneration and love, from a retreat which I had chosen with the fondest predilection, and in my flattering hopes with an immutable decision as the asylum of my declining years; a retreat which was rendered every day more necessary as well as more dear to me, by the addition of habit to inclination, and of frequent interruptions in my health to the gradual waste committed on it by time.

On the other hand, the magnitude and difficulty of the trust to which the voice of my country called me being sufficient to awaken in the wisest and most experienced of her citizens a distrustful scrutiny into his qualifications, could not but overwhelm with despondence one who, inheriting inferior endowments from nature, and unpracticed in the duties of civil administration, ought to be peculiarly conscious of his own deficiencies. In this conflict of emotions, all I dare aver is, that it has been my faithful study to collect my duty from a just appreciation of every circumstance by which it might be affected. All I dare hope is, that if, in executing this task, I have been too much swayed by a grateful remembrance of former instances, or by any affectionate sensibility to this transcendent proof of the confidence of my fellow-citizens, and have thence too little consulted my incapacity as well as disinclination, for the weighty and untried cares before me, my error will be palliated by the motives which misled me, and its consequences be judged by my country with some share of the partiality with which they originated.

Such being the impressions under which I have, in obedience to the public summons, repaired to the present station, it would be peculiarly improper to omit in this first official act, my fervent supplications to that Almighty Being who rules over the universe, who presides in the councils of nations, and whose providential aids can supply every human defect that his benediction may consecrate to the liberties and happiness of the people of the United States, a government instituted by themselves for these essential purposes, and may enable every instrument employed in its administration to execute with success the functions allotted to his charge. In tendering this homage to the great author of every public and private good, I assure myself that it expresses your sentiments, not less than my own, nor those of my fellow-citizens at large less than either. No people can be bound to acknowledge and adore the invisible hand which conducts the affairs of men more than the people of the United States. Every step by which they have advanced to the character of an independent nation seems to have been distinguished by some token of providential agency, and in the important revolution just accomplished in the system of their united government the tranquil deliberations and voluntary consent of so many distinct communities from which the event has resulted cannot be compared with the means by which most governments have been established without some return of pious gratitude along with a humble anticipation of the future blessings which the past seem to presage. These reflections arising out of the present crisis have forced themselves too strongly on my mind to be suppressed. You will join with me, I trust, in thinking that there are none under the influence of which the proceedings of a new and free government can more auspiciously commence.

By the article establishing the executive department it is made the duty of the President "to recommend to your consideration such measures as he shall judge necessary and expedient." The circumstances under which I now meet you will acquit me from entering into that subject farther than to refer to the great constitutional charter under which you are assembled, and which in defining your powers designates the objects to which your attention is to be given. It will be more consistent with those circumstances, and far more congenial with the feelings which actuate me to substitute in place of a recommendation of particular measures, the tribute that is due to the talents, the rectitude, and the patriotism which adorn the characters selected to devise and adopt them. In these honorable qualifications, I behold the surest pledges that as on one side no local prejudices or attachments, no separate views, no party animosities will misdirect the comprehensive and equal eye which ought to watch over this great assemblage of communities and interests, so on another, that the foundations of our national policy will be laid in the pure and immutable principles of private morality, and the pre-eminence of free government be exemplified by all the attributes which can win the affections of its citizens and command the respect of the world. I dwell on this prospect with every satisfaction which an ardent love for my country can inspire, since there is no truth more thoroughly established than that there exists in the economy and course of nature, an indissoluble union between virtue and happiness, between duty and advantage, between the genuine maxims of an honest and magnanimous policy and the solid rewards of the public prosperity and felicity. Since we ought to be no less persuaded that the propitious smiles of heaven can never be expected on a nation that disregards the eternal rules of order and right which heaven itself has ordained, and since the preservation of the sacred fire of Liberty, and the destiny of the republican model of government are justly considered as deeply, perhaps as finally staked on the experiment entrusted to the hands of the American people. Besides the ordinary objects submitted to your care, it will remain with your judgment to decide how far an exercise of the occasional power delegated by the fifth article of the Constitution is rendered expedient at the present juncture by the nature of the objections which have been urged against the system, or by the degree of inquietude which has given birth to them. Instead of undertaking particular recommendations on this subject in which I could be guided by no lights derived from official opportunities, I shall again give way to my entire confidence in your discernment aud pursuit of the public good, for I assure myself that while you carefully avoid every alteration which might endanger the benefits of an united and effective government, or which ought to await the future lessons of experience, a reverence for the characteristic rights of freemen, and a regard for the public harmony will sufficiently influence your deliberations on the question, how far the former can be more impregnably fortified, or the latter be safely and advantageously promoted.

To the preceding observations I have one to add, which will be most properly addressed to the House of Representatives. It concerns myself, and will, therefore, be as brief as possible. When I was first honored with a call into the service of my country, then on the eve of an arduous struggle for its liberties, the light in which I comtemplated my duty required that I should renounce every pecuniary compensation. From this resolution I have in no instance departed, and being still under the impressions which produced it, I must decline as inapplicable to myself any share in the personal emoluments which may be indispensably included in a permanent provision for the executive department, and must accordingly pray that the pecuniary estimates for the station in which I am placed, may, during my continuance in it, be limited to such actual expenditures as the public good may be thought to require.

Having thus imparted to you my sentiments, as as they have been awakened by the occasion which brings us together, I shall take my present leave, but not without resorting once more to the benign parent of the human race in humble supplication, that since he has been pleased to favor the American people with opportunities for deliberating in perfect tranquillity, and dispositions for deciding with unparalleled unanimity on a form of government for the security of their union and the advancement of their happiness, so His divine blessing may be equally conspicuous in the enlarged views, the temperate consultations, and the wise measures on which the success of this government must depend.

WASHINGTON'S FAREWELL ADDRESS.

FRIENDS AND FELLOW-CITIZENS—The period for a new election of a citizen to administer the executive government of the United States not being far distant, and the time actually arrived when your thoughts must be employed in designating the person who is to be clothed with that important trust, it appears to me proper, especially as it may conduce to a more distinct expression of the public voice, that I should now apprise you of the resolution I have formed, to decline being considered among the number of those out of whom a choice is to be made.

I beg you, at the same time, to do me the justice to be assured that this resolution has not been taken without a strict regard to all the considerations appertaining to the relation which binds a dutiful citizen to his country; and that, in withdrawing the tender of service which silence, in my situation, might imply, I am influenced by no diminution of zeal for your future interest, no deficiency of grateful respect for your past kindness, but am supported by a full conviction that the step is compatible with both.

The acceptance of, and continuance hitherto in, the office to which your suffrages have twice called me, have been a uniform sacrifice of inclination to the opinion of duty, and to a deference for what appeared to be your desire. I constantly hoped that it would have been much earlier in my power, consistently with motives which I was not at liberty to disregard, to return to that retirement from which I had been reluctantly drawn. The strength of my inclination to do this, previous to the last election, had been led to the preparation of an address to declare it to you; but mature reflection on the then perplexed and critical posture of our affairs with foreign nations, and the unanimous advice of persons entitled to my confidence, impelled me to abandon the idea.

I rejoice that the state of your concerns, external as well as internal, no longer renders the pursuit of inclination incompatible with the sentiment of duty or propriety; and am persuaded, whatever partiality may be retained for my services, that, in the present circumstances of our country, you will not disapprove my determination to retire.

The impressions with which I first undertook the arduous trust were explained on the proper occasion. In the discharge of this trust, I will only say, that I have with good intentions contributed toward the organization and administration of the government the best exertions of which a very fallible judgment was capable. Not unconscious in the outset of the inferiority of my qualifications, experience, in my own eyes—perhaps still more in the eyes of others—has strengthened the motives to diffidence of myself; and every day the increasing weight of years admonishes me, more and more, that the shade of retirement is as necessary to me as it will be welcome. Satisfied that, if any circumstances have given peculiar value to my services, they were temporary, I have the consolation to believe that, while choice and prudence invite me to quit the political scene, patriotism does not forbid it.

In looking forward to the moment which is intended to terminate the career of my public life, my feelings do not permit me to suspend the deep acknowledgment of that debt of gratitude which I owe to my beloved country for the many honors it has conferred upon me; still more for the steadfast confidence with which it has supported me, and for the opportunities I have thence enjoyed of manifesting my inviolable attachment, by services faithful and persevering, though in usefulness unequal to my zeal. If benefits have resulted to our country from these services, let it always be remembered to your praise, and as an instructive example in our annals, that, under circumstances in which the passions, agitated in every direction, were liable to mislead; amid appearances sometimes dubious, vicissitudes of fortune often discouraging; in situations in which, not unfrequently, want of success has countenanced the spirit of criticism—the constancy of your support was the essential prop of the efforts, and a guarantee of the plans by which they were effected. Profoundly penetrated with this idea, I shall carry it with me to my grave, as a strong incitement to unceasing vows that Heaven may continue to you the choicest tokens of its beneficence; that your union and brotherly affection may be perpetual; that the free constitution, which is the work of your hands, may be sacredly maintained; that its administration, in every department, may be stamped with wisdom and virtue; that, in fine, the happiness of the people of these States, under the auspices of liberty, may be made complete, by so careful a preservation and so prudent a use of this blessing as will acquire to them the glory of recommending it to the applause, the affection, and the adoption of every nation which is yet a stranger to it.

Here, perhaps, I ought to stop; but a solicitude for your welfare, which can not end but with my life, and the apprehension of danger natural to that solicitude, urge me, on an occasion like the present to offer to your solemn contemplation, and to recommend to your frequent review, some sentiments, which are the result of much reflection, of no inconsiderable observation, and which appear to me all-important to the permanency of your felicity as a people. These will be afforded to you with the more freedom, as you can only see them in the disinterested warnings of a parting friend, who can possibly have no personal motive to bias his counsel; nor can I forget, as an encouragement to it, your indulgent reception of my sentiments on a former and not dissimilar occasion.

Interwoven as is the love of liberty with every ligament of your hearts, no recommendation of mine is necessary to fortify or confirm the attachment.

The unity of government, which constitutes you one people, is also now dear to you. It is justly so; for it is a main pillar in the edifice of your real independence, the support of your tranquillity at home, your peace abroad, of your safety, of your prosperity, of that very liberty which you so highly prize. But as it is easy to forsee that from different causes and from different quarters much pains will be taken, many artifices employed, to weaken in your minds the conviction of this truth—as this is the point in your political fortress against which the batteries of internal and external enemies will be most constantly and actively (though often covertly and insidiously) directed—it is of infinite moment that you should properly estimate the immense value of your national union to your collective and individual happiness; that you should cherish a cordial, habitual, and immovable attachment to it, accustoming yourselves to think and speak of it as of the palladium of your political safety and prosperity; watching for its preservation with jealous anxiety; discountenancing whatever may suggest even a suspicion that it can, in any event, be abandoned; and indignantly frowning upon the first dawning of every attempt to alienate any portion of our country from the rest, or to enfeeble the sacred ties which now link together the various parts.

For this you have every inducement of sympathy and interest. Citizens, by birth or choice of a common country, that country has a right to concentrate your affections. The name of *American*, which belongs to you in your national capacity, must always exalt the just pride of patriotism more than any appellation derived from local discriminations. With slight shades of difference, you have the same religion, manners, habits, and political principles. You have, in a common cause, fought and triumphed together; the independence and liberty you possess are the work of joint counsels and joint efforts, of common dangers, sufferings, and successes.

But these considerations, however powerfully they address themselves to your sensibility, are greatly outweighed by those which apply more immediately to your interest; here every portion of our country finds the most commanding motives for carefully guarding and preserving the union of the whole.

The North, in an unrestrained intercourse with the South, protected by the equal laws of a common government, finds, in the productions of the latter, great additional resources of maritime and commercial enterprise, and precious materials of manufacturing industry. The South, in the same intercourse, benefiting by the agency of the North, sees its agriculture grow and its commerce expand. Turning partly into its own channels the seamen of the North, it finds its particular navigation invigorated; and while it contributes, in different ways, to nourish and increase the general mass of the national navigation, it looks forward to the protection of a maritime strength to which itself is unequally adapted. The

East, in like intercourse with the West, already finds, and, in the progressive improvement of interior communication, by land and water, will more and more find, a valuable vent for the commodities which it brings from abroad or manufactures at home. The West derives from the East supplies requisite for its growth and comfort, and, what is perhaps of still greater consequence, it must, of necessity, owe the secure enjoyment of indispensable outlets for its own productions to the weight, influence, and the future maritime strength of the Atlantic side of the Union, directed by an indissoluble community of interest as one nation. Any other tenure by which the West can hold this essential advantage, whether derived from its own separate strength or from an apostate and unnatural connection with any foreign power, must be intrinsically precarious.

While, then, every part of our country thus feels an immediate and particular interest in union, all the parts combined can not fail to find, in the united mass of means and efforts, greater strength, greater resource, proportionably greater security from external danger, a less frequent interruption of their peace by foreign nations, and, what is of inestimable value, they must derive from union an exemption from those broils and wars between themselves, which so frequently afflict neighboring countries, not tied together by the same government, which their own rivalships alone would be sufficient to produce, but which opposite foreign alliances, attachments, and intrigues would stimulate and embitter. Hence, likewise, they will avoid the necessity of those overgrown military establishments, which, under any form of government, are inauspicious to liberty, and which are to be regarded as particularly hostile to republican liberty; in this sense it is that your union ought to be considered as the main prop of your liberty, and that the love of the one ought to endear to you the preservation of the other.

These considerations speak a persuasive language to every reflecting and virtuous mind, and exhibit a continuance of the Union as a primary object of patriotic desire. Is there a doubt whether a common government can embrace so large a sphere? Let experience solve it. To listen to mere speculation, in such a case, were criminal. We are authorized to hope that a proper organization of the whole, with the auxiliary agency of governments for the respective subdivisions, will afford a happy issue to the experiment. It is well worth a full and fair experiment. With such powerful and obvious motives to union, affecting all parts of our country, while experience shall not have demonstrated its impracticability, there will always be reason to distrust the patriotism of those who, in any quarter, may endeavor to weaken its bands.

In contemplating the causes which may disturb our Union, it occurs, as a matter of serious concern, that any ground should have been furnished for characterizing parties by geographical discriminations—Northern and Southern, Atlantic and Western—whence designing men may endeavor to excite a belief that there is real difference of local interests and views. One of the expedients of party to acquire influence within particular districts is to misrepresent the opinions and aims of other districts. You can not shield yourselves too much against the jealousies and heart-burnings which spring from these misrepresentations; they tend to render alien to each other those who ought to be bound together by fraternal affection. The inhabitants of our Western country have lately had a useful lesson on this head; they have seen in the negotiation by the Executive, and in the unanimous ratification by the Senate, of the treaty with Spain, and in the universal satisfaction at that event throughout the United States, a decisive proof how unfounded were the suspicions propagated among them, of a policy in the general government, and in the Atlantic States, unfriendly to their interests in regard to the Mississippi; they have been witnesses to the formation of two treaties—that with

Great Britain and that with Spain—which secure to them everything they could desire in respect to our foreign relations, toward confirming their prosperity. Will it not be their wisdom to rely for the preservation of these advantages on the Union by which they were procured? Will they not henceforth be deaf to those advisers, if such there are, who would sever them from their brethren and connect them with aliens?

To the efficacy and permanency of your Union, a government for the whole is indispensable. No alliance, however strict, between the parts, can be an adequate substitute; they must inevitably experience the infractions and interruptions which all alliances, in all time, have experienced. Sensible of this momentous truth, you have improved upon your first essay, by the adoption of a constitution of government better calculated than your former for an intimate Union, and for the efficacious management of your common concerns. This government, the offspring of your own choice, uninfluenced and unawed, adopted upon full investigation and mature deliberation, completely free in its principles, in the distribution of its powers, uniting security with energy, and containing within itself a provision for its own amendment, has a just claim to your confidence and your support. Respect for its authority, compliance with its laws, acquiescence in its measures, are duties enjoined by the fundamental maxims of liberty. The basis of our political systems is the right of the people to make and to alter their constitutions of government; but the constitution which at any time exists, till changed by an explicit and and authentic act of the whole people, is sacredly obligatory upon all. The very idea of the power and the right of the people to establish government presupposes the duty of every individual to obey the established government.

All obstructions to the execution of the laws, all combinations and associations, under whatever plausible character, with the real design to direct, control, counteract, or awe the regular deliberation and action of the constituted authorities, are destructive to this fundamental principle, and of fatal tendency. They serve to organize faction, to give it an artificial and extraordinary force, to put in the place of the delegated will of the nation the will of a party—often a small but artful and enterprising minority of the community—and, according to the alternate triumphs of different parties, to make the public administration the mirror of the ill-concerted and incongruous projects of faction rather than the organ of consistent and wholesome plans, digested by common counsels, and modified by mutual interests.

However combinations or associations of the above description may now and then answer popular ends, they are likely, in the course of time and things, to become potent engines, by which cunning, ambitious, and unprincipled men will be enabled to subvert the power of the people, and to usurp for themselves the reins of government; destroying, afterward, the very engine which had lifted them to unjust dominion.

Toward the preservation of your government, and the permanency of your present happy state, it is requisite, not only that you steadily discountenance irregular oppositions to its acknowledged authority, but also that you resist with care the spirit of innovation upon its principles, however specious the pretexts. One method of assault may be to effect, in the forms of the constitution, alterations which will impair the energy of the system, and thus to undermine what cannot be directly overthrown. In all the changes to which you may be invited, remember that time and habit are at least as necessary to fix the true character of governments as of other human institutions; that experience is the surest standard by which to test the real tendency of the existing constitution of a country; that facility in changes, upon the credit of mere hypothesis and opinion, exposes to perpetual change, from the endless variety of hypothesis and opinion; and remember, especially, that for the efficient management of your common interests, in a country so extensive as ours, a government of as much vigor as is consistent with the perfect security of liberty is indispensable. Liberty itself will find in such a government, with powers properly distributed and adjusted, its surest guardian. It is, indeed, little else than a name, where the government is too feeble to withstand the enterprises of faction, to confine each member of the society within the limits prescribed by the laws, and to maintain all in the secure and tranquil enjoyment of the rights of person and property.

I have already intimated to you the danger of parties in the state, with particular reference to the founding of them on geographical discriminations. Let me now take a more comprehensive view, and warn you, in the most solemn manner, against the baneful effects of the spirit of party generally.

This spirit, unfortunately, is inseparable from our nature, having its root in the strongest passions of the human mind. It exists, under different shapes, in all governments, more or less stifled, controlled, or repressed; but in those of the popular form it is seen in its greatest rankness, and is truly their worst enemy.

The alternate domination of one faction over another, sharpened by the spirit of revenge, natural to party dissension, which, in different ages and countries, has perpetrated the most horrid enormities, is itself a frightful despotism. But this leads, at length, to a more formal and permanent despotism. The disorders and miseries which result gradually incline the minds of men to seek security and repose in the absolute power of an individual; and, sooner or later, the chief of some prevailing faction, more able or more fortunate than his competitors, turns this disposition to the purposes of his own elevation on the ruins of public liberty.

Without looking forward to an extremity of this kind (which, nevertheless, ought not to be entirely out of sight), the common and continued mischiefs of the spirit of party are sufficient to make it the interest and duty of a wise people to discourage and restrain it.

It serves always to distract the public councils and enfeeble the public administration. It agitates the community with ill-founded jealousies and false alarms; kindles the animosity of one part against another; foments, occasionally, riot and insurrection. It opens the door to foreign influence and corruption, which find a facilitated access to the government itself through the channels of party passions. Thus the policy and the will of one country are subjected to the policy and will of another.

There is an opinion that parties, in free countries, are useful checks upon the administration of the government, and serve to keep alive the spirit of liberty. This, within certain limits, is probably true; and in governments of a monarchial cast, patriotism may look with indulgence, if not with favor, upon the spirit of party. But in those of the popular character, in governments purely elective, it is a spirit not to be encouraged. From their natural tendency, it is certain there will always be enough of that spirit for every salutatory purpose. And there being constant danger of excess, the effort ought to be by force of public opinion to mitigate and assuage it. A fire not to be quenched, it demands a uniform vigilance to prevent its bursting into a flame, lest, instead of warming, it should consume.

It is important, likewise, that the habits of thinking, in a free country, should inspire caution in those intrusted with its administration, to confine themselves within their respective constitutional spheres, avoiding, in the exercise of the powers of one department, to encroach upon another. The spirit of encroachment tends to consolidate the powers of all the departments into one, and thus to create, whatever the form of government, a real despotism. A just estimate of that love of power and proneness to abuse it which predominate in the human heart is sufficient to satisfy us of the truth of this position. The necessity of reciprocal checks in the exercise of political power, by dividing and distributing it into different depositories, and constituting each the guardian of the public weal, against invasion by the others, has been evinced by experiments, ancient and modern—some of them in our own country and under our own eyes. To preserve them must be as necessary as to institute them. If, in the opinion of the people, the distribution or modification of the constitutional powers be, in any particular, wrong, let it be corrected by an amendment in the way which the constitution designates. But let there be no change by usurpation; for though this, in one instance, may be the instrument of good, it is the customary weapon by which free governments are destroyed. The precedent must always greatly overbalance, in permanent evil, any partial or transient benefit which the use can, at any time, yield.

Of all the dispositions and habits which lead to political prosperity, religion and morality are indispensable supports. In vain would that man claim the tribute of patriotism who should labor to subvert these great pillars of human happiness, these firmest props of the duties of men and citizens. The mere politician, equally with the pious man, ought to respect and to cherish them. A volume could not trace all their connections with private and public felicity. Let it simply be asked, Where is the security for property, for reputation, for life, if the sense of religious obligation *desert* the oaths which are the instruments of investigation in courts of justice? And let us with caution indulge the supposition that morality can be maintained without religion. Whatever may be conceded to the influence of refined education on minds of peculiar structure, reason and experience both forbid us to expect that national morality can prevail in exclusion of religious principles.

It is substantially true, that virtue or morality is a necessary spring of popular government. The rule, indeed, extends with more or less force to every species of free government. Who that is a sincere friend to it can look with indifference upon attempts to shake the foundation of the fabric?

Promote, then, as an object of primary importance, institutions for the general diffusion of knowledge. In proportion as a structure of a government gives force to public opinion, it is essential that public opinion should be enlightened.

As a very important source of strength and security, cherish public credit. One method of preserving it is to use it as sparingly as possible;

avoiding occasions of expense by cultivating peace, but remembering, also, that timely disbursements to prepare for danger frequently prevent much greater disbursements to repel it; avoiding, likewise, the accumulation of debt, not only by shunning occasions of expense, but by vigorous exertions in time of peace to discharge the debts which unavoidable wars may have occasioned; not ungenerously throwing upon posterity the burden which we ourselves ought to bear. The execution of these maxims belongs to your representatives, but it is necessary that public opinion should coöperate. To facilitate to them the performance of their duty, it is essential that you should practically bear in mind that toward the payment of debts there must be revenue; that to have revenue there must be taxes; that no taxes can be devised which are not more or less inconvenient and unpleasant; that the intrinsic embarrassment inseparable from the selection of the proper objects (which is always a choice of difficulties), ought to be a decisive motive for a candid construction of the conduct of the government in making it, and for a spirit of acquiescence in the measures for obtaining revenue which the public exigencies may at any time dictate.

Observe good faith and justice toward all nations; cultivate peace and harmony with all; religion and morality enjoin this conduct, and can it be that good policy does not really enjoin it? It will be worthy of a free, enlightened, and, at no distant period, a great nation, to give to mankind the magnanimous and too novel example of a people always guided by an exalted justice and benevolence. Who can doubt that, in the course of time and things, the fruits of such a plan would richly repay any temporary advantages which might be lost by a steady adherence to it? Can it be that Providence has not connected the permanent felicity of a nation with its virtue? The experiment, at least, is recommended by every sentiment which ennobles human nature. Alas! it is rendered impossible by its vices?

In the execution of such a plan, nothing is more essential than that permanent inveterate antipathies against particular nations, and passionate attachments for others, should be excluded, and that, in place of them, just and amicable feelings toward all should be cultivated. The nation which indulges toward another an habitual hatred, or an habitual fondness, is, in some degree, a slave. It is a slave to its animosity or its affection, either of which is sufficient to lead it astray from its duty and its interest. Antipathy in one nation against another disposes each more readily to offer insult and injury, to lay hold of slight causes of umbrage, and to be haughty and intractable when accidental or trifling occasions of dispute occur. Hence, frequent collisions, obstinate, envenomed, and bloody contests. The nation, prompted by ill-will and resentment, sometimes impels to war the government, contrary to the best calculations of policy. The government sometimes participates in the national propensity, and adopts, through passion, what reason would reject; at other times it makes the animosity of the nation subservient to projects of hostility, instigated by pride, ambition, and other sinister and pernicious motives. The peace often, sometimes perhaps the liberty of nations, has been the victim.

So, likewise, a passionate attachment of one nation to another produces a variety of evils. Sympathy for the favorite nation, facilitating the illusion of an imaginary common interest, in cases where no real common interest exists, and infusing into one the enmities of the other, betrays the former into a participation into the quarrels and wars of the latter, without adequate inducement or justification. It leads also to concessions to the favorite nation of privileges denied to others, which is apt doubly to injure the nation making the concessions, by unnecessarily parting with what ought to have been retained, and by exciting jealousy, ill-will, and a disposition to retaliate, in the parties from whom equal privileges are withheld; and it gives to ambitious, corrupted, or deluded citizens (who devote themselves to the favorite nation), facility to betray or sacrifice the interest of their own country, without odium, sometimes even with popularity; gilding with the appearance of a virtuous sense of obligation, a commendable deference for public opinion, or a laudable zeal for public good, the base or foolish compliances of ambition, corruption, or infatuation.

As avenues to foreign influence in innumerable ways, such attachments are particularly alarming to the truly enlightened and independent patriot. How many opportunities do they afford to tamper with domestic factions, to practice the art of seduction, to mislead public opinion, to influence or awe the public councils! Such an attachment of a small or weak toward a great and powerful nation dooms the former to be the satellite of the latter.

Against the insidious wiles of foreign influence (I conjure you to believe me, fellow-citizens) the jealousy of a free people ought to be *constantly* awake, since history and experience prove that foreign influence is one of the most baneful foes of republican government. But that jealousy, to be useful, must be impartial, else it becomes the instrument of the very influence to be avoided, instead of a defense against it. Excessive partiality for one foreign nation, and excessive dislike for another, cause those whom they actuate to see danger only on one side, and serve to vail, and even second, the arts of influence on the other. Real patriots, who may resist the intrigues of the favorite, are liable to become suspected and odious, while its tools and dupes usurp the applause and confidence of the people, to surrender their interests.

The great rule of conduct for us, in regard to foreign nations, is, in extending our commercial relations, to have with them as little political connection as possible. So far as we have already formed engagements, let them be fulfilled with perfect good faith. Here let us stop.

Europe has a set of primary interests, which to us have none or a very remote relation. Hence she must be engaged in frequent controversies, the causes of which are essentially foreign to our concerns. Hence, therefore, it must be unwise in us to implicate ourselves, by artificial ties, in the ordinary vicissitudes of her politics, or the ordinary combinations and collisions of her friendships or enmities.

Our detached and distant situation invites and enables us to pursue a different course. If we remain one people, under an efficient government, the period is not far off when we may defy material injury from external annoyance, when we may take such an attitude as will cause the neutrality we may at any time resolve upon to be scrupulously respected —when belligerent nations, under the impossibility of making acquisitions upon us, will not lightly hazard the giving us provocation—when we may choose peace or war, as our interest, guided by justice, shall counsel.

Why forego the advantages of so peculiar a situation? Why quit our own to stand upon foreign ground? Why, by interweaving our destiny with that of any part of Europe, entangle our peace and prosperity in the toils of European ambition, rivalship, interest, humor, or caprice?

It is our true policy to steer clear of permanent alliances with any portion of the foreign world; so far, I mean, as we are now at liberty to do it; for let me not be understood as capable of patronizing infidelity to existing engagements. I hold the maxim no less applicable to public than to private affairs, that honesty is always the best policy. I repeat it, therefore, let those engagements be observed in their genuine sense. But, in my opinion, it is unnecessary, and would be unwise, to extend them.

Taking care always to keep ourselves, by suitable establishments, on a respectable defensive posture, we may safely trust to temporary alliances for extraordinary emergencies.

Harmony, and a liberal intercourse with all nations, are recommended by policy, humanity, and interest. But even our commercial policy should hold an equal and impartial hand; neither seeking nor granting exclusive favors or preferences; consulting the natural course of things; diffusing and diversifying, by gentle means, the streams of commerce, but forcing nothing; establishing, with powers so disposed, in order to give trade a stable course, to define the rights of our merchants, and to enable the government to support them, conventional rules of intercourse, the best that present circumstances and mutual opinions will permit, but temporary, and liable to be, from time to time, abandoned or varied, as experience and circumstances shall dictate; constantly keeping in view that it is folly in one nation to look for disinterested favors from another; that it must pay, with a portion of its independence, for whatever it may accept under that character; that by such acceptance it may place itself in the condition of having given equivalents for nominal favors, and yet of being reproached with ingratitude for not giving more. There can be no greater error than to expect, or calculate upon, real favors from nation to nation.

It is an illusion which experience must cure, which a just pride ought to discard.

In offering to you, my countrymen, these counsels of an old and affectionate friend, I dare not hope they will make the strong and lasting impression I could wish—that they will control the usual current of the passions, or prevent our nation from running the course which has hitherto marked the destiny of nations; but if I may even flatter myself that they may be productive of some partial benefit, some occasional good, that they may now and then recur to moderate the fury of party spirit, to warn against the mischiefs of foreign intrigues, to guard against the impostures of pretended patriotism—this hope will be a full recompense for the solicitude for your welfare by which they have been dictated.

How far, in the discharge of my official duties, I have been guided by the principles which have been delineated, the public records, and other evidences of my conduct, must witness to you and the world. To myself, the assurance of my own conscience is, that I have at least believed myself to be guided by them.

In relation to the still subsisting war in Europe, my proclamation of the 22d of April, 1793, is the index to my plan. Sanctioned by your approving voice, and by that of your representatives in both

Houses of Congress, the spirit of that measure has continually governed me, uninfluenced by any attempts to deter or divert me from it.

After deliberate examination, with the aid of the best lights I could obtain, I was well satisfied that our country, under all the circumstances of the case, had a right to take, and was bound in duty and interest to take, a neutral position. Having taken it, I determined, as far as should depend upon me, to maintain it with moderation, perseverance, and firmness.

The considerations which respect the right to hold this conduct, it is not necessary on this occasion to detail. I will only observe that, according to my understanding of the matter, that right, so far from being denied by any of the belligerent powers, has been virtually admitted by all.

The duty of holding a neutral conduct may be inferred, without anything more, from the obligation which justice and humanity impose on every nation, in cases in which it is free to act, to maintain inviolate the relations of peace and amity toward other nations.

The inducements of interest, for observing that conduct, will be best referred to your own reflections and experience. With me, a predominant motive has been to endeavor to gain time to our country to settle and mature its yet recent institutions, and to progress, without interruption, to that degree of strength and consistency which is necessary to give it, humanly speaking, the command of its own fortunes.

Though, in reviewing the incidents of my administration, I am unconscious of intentional error, I am, nevertheless, too sensible of my defects not to think it probable that I may have committed many errors. Whatever they may be, I fervently beseech the Almighty to avert or mitigate the evils to which they may tend. I shall also carry with me the hope that my country will never cease to view them with indulgence, and that, after forty-five years of my life dedicated to its service with an upright zeal, the faults of incompetent abilities will be consigned to oblivion, as myself must soon be to the mansions of rest.

Relying on its kindness in this, as in other things, and actuated by that fervent love toward it which is so natural to a man who views in it the native soil of himself and his progenitors for several generations, I anticipate, with pleasing expectation, that retreat in which I promise myself to realize, without alloy, the sweet enjoyment of partaking, in the midst of my fellow-citizens, the benign influence of good laws under a free government—the ever favorite object of my heart—and the happy reward, as I trust, of our mutual cares, labors, and dangers.

George Washington.

United States, *17th September*, 1796.

PRESIDENT JACKSON'S PROCLAMATION,

ISSUED IN 1832, WHEN SOUTH CAROLINA UNDERTOOK TO ANNUL THE FEDERAL REVENUE LAW.

Whereas a convention, assembled in the State of South Carolina, have passed an ordinance, by which they declare "that the several acts and parts of acts of the Congress of the United States, purporting to be laws for the imposing of duties and imposts on the importation of foreign commodities, and now having actual operation and effect within the United States, and more especially 'two acts for the same purposes, passed on the 29th of May, 1828, and on the 14th of July, 1832,' are unauthorized by the Constitution of the United States, and violate the true meaning and intent thereof, and are null and void, and no law," nor binding on the citizens of that State or its officers; and by the said ordinance it is further declared to be unlawful for any of the constituted authorities of the State, or of the United States, to enforce the payment of the duties imposed by the said acts within the same State, and that it is the duty of the legislature to pass such laws as may be necessary to give full effect to the said ordinances:

And whereas, by the said ordinance it is further ordained, that, in no case of law or equity, decided in the courts of said State, wherein shall be drawn in question the validity of the said ordinance, or of the acts of the legislature that may be passed to give it effect, or of the said laws of the United States, no appeal shall be allowed to the Supreme Court of the United States, nor shall any copy of the record be permitted or allowed for that purpose; and that any person attempting to take such appeal, shall be punished as for a contempt of court:

And, finally, the said ordinance declares that the people of South Carolina will maintain the said ordinance at every hazard; and that they will consider the passage of any act by Congress abolishing or closing the ports of the said State, or otherwise obstructing the free ingress or egress of vessels to and from the said ports, or any other act of the Federal Government to coerce the State, shut up her ports, destroy or harass her commerce, or to enforce the said acts otherwise than through the civil tribunals of the country, as inconsistent with the longer continuance of South Carolina in the Union; and that the people of the said State will thenceforth hold themselves absolved from all further obligation to maintain or preserve their political connection with the people of the other States, and will forthwith proceed to organize a separate government, and do all other acts and things which sovereign and independent States may of right do:

And whereas the said ordinance prescribes to the people of South Carolina a course of conduct in direct violation of their duty as citizens of the United States, contrary to the laws of their country, subversive of its Constitution, and having for its object the destruction of the Union—that Union, which, coeval with our political existence, led our fathers, without any other ties to unite them than those of patriotism and common cause, through a sanguinary struggle to a glorious independence—that sacred Union, hitherto, inviolate, which, perfected by our happy Constitution, has brought us, by the favor of Heaven, to a state of prosperity at home, and high consideration abroad, rarely, if ever, equaled in the history of nations; to preserve this bond of our political existence from destruction, to maintain inviolate this state of national honor and prosperity, and to justify the confidence my fellow-citizens have reposed in me, I, Andrew Jackson, President of the United States, have thought proper to issue this, my PROCLAMATION, stating my views of the Constitution and laws applicable to the measures adopted by the Convention of South Carolina, and to the reasons they have put forth to sustain them, declaring the course which duty will require me to pursue, and, appealing to the understanding and patriotism of the people, warn them of the consequences that must inevitably result from an observance of the dictates of the Convention.

Strict duty would require of me nothing more than the exercise of those powers with which I am now, or may hereafter be, invested, for preserving the Union, and for the execution of the laws. But the imposing aspect which opposition has assumed in this case, by clothing itself with State authority, and the deep interest which the people of the United States must all feel in preventing a resort to stronger measures, while there is a hope that anything will be yielded to reasoning and remonstrances, perhaps demand, and will certainly justify, a full exposition to South Carolina and the nation of the views I entertain of this important question, as well as a distinct enunciation of the course which my sense of duty will require me to pursue.

The ordinance is founded, not on the indefeasible right of resisting acts which are plainly unconstitutional, and too oppressive to be endured, but on the strange position that any one State may not only declare an act of Congress void, but prohibit its execution—that they may do this consistently with the Constitution—that the true construction of that instrument permits a State to retain its place in the Union, and yet be bound by no other of its laws than those it may choose to consider as constitutional. It is true they add, that, to justify this abrogation of a law, it must be palpably contrary to the Constitution; but it is evident, that to give the right of resisting laws of that description, coupled with the uncontrolled right to decide what laws deserve that character, is to give the power of resisting all laws. For, as by the theory, there is no appeal, the reasons alleged by the State, good or bad, must prevail. If it should be said that public opinion is a sufficient check against the abuse of this power, it may be asked why is it not deemed a sufficient guard against the passage of an unconstitutional act by Congress. There is, however, a restraint in this last case, which makes the assumed power of a State more indefensible, and which does not exist in the other. There are two appeals from an unconstitutional act passed by Congress—one to the judiciary, the other to the people and the States. There is no appeal from the State decision in theory; and the practical illustration shows that the courts are closed against an application to review it, both judges and jurors being sworn to decide in its favor. But reasoning on this subject is superfluous, when our social compact in express terms declares, that the laws of the United States, its Constitution, and treaties made under it, are the supreme law of the land; and for greater caution adds, "that the judges in every State shall be bound thereby, anything in the constitution or laws of any State to the contrary notwithstanding." And it may be asserted, without fear of refutation, that no federative government could exist without a similar provision. Look, for a moment, to the consequence. If South Carolina considers the revenue laws unconstitutional, and has a right to prevent their execution in the port of Charleston, there would be a clear constitutional objection to their collection in every other port, and no revenue could be collected anywhere; for all imposts must be equal. It is no answer to repeat that an unconstitutional law is no law, so long as the question of its legality is to be decided by the State itself; for every law operating injuriously upon any local interest will be perhaps thought, and certainly represented, as unconstitutional, and, as has been shown, there is no appeal.

If this doctrine had been established at an earlier day, the Union would have been dissolved in its infancy. The excise law in Pennsylvania, the embargo and non-intercourse law in the Eastern States, the carriage tax in Virginia, were all deemed unconstitutional, and were more unequal in their operation than any of the laws now complained of; but, fortunately, none of those States discovered that they had the right now claimed by South Carolina. The war into which we were forced, to support the dignity of the nation and the rights of our citizens, might have ended in defeat and disgrace, instead of victory and honor, if the States, who supposed it a ruinous and unconstitutional measure, had thought they possessed the right of nullifying the act by which it was declared, and denying supplies for its prosecution. Hardly and unequally as those measures bore upon several members of the Union, to the legislatures of none did this efficient and peaceable remedy, as it is called, suggest itself. The discovery of this important feature in our Constitution was reserved to the present day. To the statesmen of South Carolina belongs the invention, and upon the citizens of that State will, unfortunately, fall the evils of reducing it to practice.

If the doctrine of a State veto upon the laws of the Union carries with it internal evidence of its impracticable absurdity, our constitutional history will also afford abundant proof that it would have been repudiated with indignation had it been proposed to form a feature in our government.

In our colonial state, although dependent on another power, we very early considered ourselves as connected by common interest with each other. Leagues were formed for common defense, and before the Declaration of Independence, we were known in our aggregate character as the United Colonies of America. That decisive and important step was taken jointly. We declared ourselves a nation by a joint, not by several acts; and when the terms of our confederation were reduced to form, it was in that of a solemn league of several States, by which they agreed that they would, collectively, form one nation, for the purpose of conducting some certain domestic concerns, and all foreign relations. In the instrument forming that Union, is found an article which declares that "every State shall abide by the determinations of Congress on all questions which by that Confederation should be submitted to them."

Under the Confederation, then, no State could legally annul a decision of the Congress, or refuse to submit to its execution; but no provision was made to enforce these decisions. Congress made requisitions, but they were not complied with. The government could not operate on individuals. They had no judiciary, no means of collecting revenue.

But the defects of the Confederation need not be detailed. Under its operation we could scarcely be called a nation. We had neither prosperity at home nor consideration abroad. This state of things could not be endured, and our present happy Constitution was formed, but formed in vain, if this fatal doctrine prevails. It was formed for important objects that are announced in the preamble made in the name and by the authority of the people of the United States, whose delegates framed, and whose conventions approved, it.

The most important among these objects, that which is placed first in rank, on which all the others rest, is "*to form a more perfect Union.*" Now, it is possible that, even if there were no express provision giving supremacy to the Constitution and laws of the United States over those of the States, it can be conceived that an instrument made for the purpose of "*forming a more perfect Union*" than that of the Confederation, could be so constructed by the assembled wisdom of our country as to substitute for that confederation a form of government, dependent for its existence on the local interest, the party spirit of a State, or of a prevailing faction in a State? Every man, of plain, unsophisticated understanding, who hears the question, will give such an answer as will preserve the Union. Metaphysical subtlety, in pursuit of an impracticable theory, could alone have devised one that is calculated to destroy it.

I consider, then, the power to annul a law of the United States, assumed by one State, *incompatible with the existence of the Union, contradicted expressly by the letter of the Constitution, unauthorized by its spirit, inconsistent with every principle on which it was founded, and destructive of the great object for which it was formed.*

After this general view of the leading principle, we must examine the particular application of it which is made in the ordinance.

The preamble rests its justification on these grounds: It assumes as a fact, that the obnoxious laws, although they purport to be laws for raising revenue, were in reality intended for the protection of manufactures, which purpose it asserts to be unconstitutional; that the operation of these laws is unequal; that the amount raised by them is greater than is required by the wants of the government; and, finally, that the proceeds are to be applied to objects unauthorized by the Constitution. These are the only causes alleged to justify an open opposition to the laws of the country, and a threat of seceding from the Union, if any attempt should be made to enforce them. The first actually acknowledges that the law in question was passed under power expressly given by the Constitution, to lay and collect imposts; but its constitutionality is drawn in question from the motives of those who passed it. However apparent this purpose may be in the present case, nothing can be more dangerous than to admit the position that an unconstitutional purpose, entertained by the members who assent to a law enacted under a constitutional power, shall make that law void; for how is that purpose to be ascertained? Who is to make the scrutiny? How often may bad purposes be falsely imputed? In how many cases are they concealed by false professions? In how many is no declaration of motive made? Admit this doctrine, and you give to the States an uncontrolled right to decide, and every law may be annulled under this pretext. If, therefore, the absurd and dangerous doctrine should be admitted, that a State may annul an unconstitutional law, or one that it deems such, it will not apply to the present case.

The next objection is, that the laws in question operate unequally. This objection may be made with truth to every law that has been or can be passed. The wisdom of man never yet contrived a system of taxation that would operate with perfect equality. If the unequal operation of a law makes it unconstitutional, and if all laws of that description may be abrogated by any State for that cause, then, indeed, is the federal Constitution unworthy of the slightest efforts for its preservation. We have hitherto relied on it as the perpetual bond of our Union. We have received it as the work of the assembled wisdom of the nation. We have trusted to it as to the sheet-anchor of our safety, in the stormy times of conflict with a foreign or domestic foe. We have looked to it with sacred awe as the palladium of our liberties, and with all the solemnities of religion have pledged to each other our lives and fortunes here, and our hopes of happiness hereafter, in its defense and support. Were we mistaken, my countrymen, in attaching this importance to the Constitution of our country? Was our devotion paid to the wretched, inefficient, clumsy contrivance, which this new doctrine would make it? Did we pledge ourselves to the support of an airy nothing—a bubble that must be blown away by the first breath of disaffection? Was this self-destroying, visionary theory the work of the profound statesmen, the exalted patriots, to whom the task of constitutional reform was intrusted? Did the name of Washington sanction, did the States deliberately ratify, such an anomaly in the history of fundamental legislation? No. We were not mistaken. The letter of this great instrument is free from this radical fault; its language directly contradicts the imputation; its spirit, its evident intent, contradicts it. No, we did not err. Our Constitution does not contain the absurdity of giving power to make laws, and another power to resist them. The sages, whose memory will always be reverenced, have given us a practical, and, as they hoped, a permanent constitutional compact. The Father of his Country did not affix his revered name to so palpable an absurdity. Nor did the States, when they severally ratified it, do so under the impression that a veto on the laws of the United States was reserved to them, or that they could exercise it by application. Search the debates in all their conventions—examine the speeches of the most zealous opposers of federal authority—look at the amendments that were proposed. They are all silent—not a syllable uttered, not a vote given, not a motion made, to correct the explicit supremacy given to the laws of the Union over those of the States, or to show that implication, as is now contended, could defeat it. No, we have not erred! The Constitution is still the object of our reverence, the bond of our union, our defense in danger, the source of our prosperity in peace. It shall descend, as we have received it, uncorrupted by sophistical construction, to our posterity; and the sacrifices of local interest, of State prejudices, of personal animosities, that were made to bring it into existence, will again be patriotically offered for its support.

The two remaining objections made by the ordinance to these laws are, that the sums intended to be raised by them are greater than are required, and that the proceeds will be unconstitutionally employed. The Constitution has given expressly to Congress the right of raising revenue, and of determining the sum the public exigencies will require. The States have no control over the exercise of this right other than that which results from the power of changing the representatives who abuse it, and thus procure redress. Congress may undoubtedly abuse this discretionary power, but the same may be said of others with which they are vested. Yet the discretion must exist somewhere. The Constitution has given it to the representatives of all the people, checked by the representatives of the States, and by the executive power. The South Carolina construction gives it to the legislature, or the convention of a single State, where neither the people of the different States, nor the States in their separate capacity, nor the chief magistrate elected by the people, have any representation. Which is the most discreet disposition of the power? I do not ask you, fellow-citizens, which is the constitutional disposition—that instrument speaks a language not to be misunderstood. But if you were assembled in general convention, which would you think the safest depository of this discretionary power in the last resort? Would you add a clause giving it to each of the States, or would you sanction the wise provisions already made by your Constitution? If this should be the result of your deliberations when providing for the future, are you—can you—be ready to risk all that we hold dear, to establish, for a temporary and a local purpose, that which you must acknowledge to be destructive, and even absurd, as a general provision? Carry out the consequences of this right vested in the different States, and you must perceive that the crisis your conduct presents at this day would recur whenever any law of the United States displeased any of the States, and that we should soon cease to be a nation.

The ordinance, with the same knowledge of the future that characterizes a former objection, tells you that the proceeds of the tax will be unconstitutionally applied. If this could be ascertained with certainty, the objection would, with more propriety, be reserved for the law so applying the proceeds, but surely can not be urged against the laws levying the duty.

These are the allegations contained in the ordinance. Examine them seriously, my fellow-citizens—judge for yourselves. I appeal to you to determine whether they are so clear, so convincing, as to leave no doubt of their correctness; and even if you should come to this conclusion, how far they justify the reckless, destructive course which you are directed to pursue. Review these objections, and the conclusions drawn from them once more. What are they? Every law, then, for raising revenue, according to the South Carolina ordinance, may be rightfully annulled, unless it be so framed as no law ever will or can be framed. Congress have a right to pass laws for raising revenue, and each State has a right to oppose their execution—two rights directly opposed to each other; and yet is this absurdity supposed to be contained in an instrument drawn for the express purpose of avoiding collisions between the States and the general government, by an assembly of the most enlightened statesmen and purest patriots ever embodied for a similiar purpose.

In vain have these sages declared that Congress shall have power to lay and collect taxes, duties, imposts, and excises—in vain have they provided that they shall have power to pass laws which shall be necessary and proper to carry those powers into execution, that those laws and that Constitution shall be the "supreme law of the land; and that the judges in every State shall be bound thereby, anything in the constitution or laws of any State to the contrary notwithstanding." In vain have the people of the several States solemnly sanctioned these provisions, made them their paramount law, and individually sworn to support them whenever they were called on to execute any office.

Vain provisions! Ineffectual restrictions! Vile profanation of oaths! Miserable mockery of legislation! If a bare majority of the voters in any one State may, on a real or supposed knowledge of the intent with which a law has been passed, declare themselves free from its operation—say here it gives too little, there too much, and operates unequally—here it suffers articles to be free that ought to be taxed, there it taxes those that ought to be free—in this case the proceeds are intended to be applied to purposes which we do not approve, in that the amount raised is more than is wanted. Congress, it is true, are invested by the Constitution with the right of deciding these questions according to their sound discretion. Congress is composed of the representatives of all the States, and of all the people of all the States; but WE, part of the people of one State, to whom the Constitution has given no power on the subject, from whom it has expressly taken it away—*we*, who have solemnly agreed that this Constitution shall be our law—*we*, most of whom have sworn to support it—*we* now abrogate this law, and swear, and force others to swear, that it shall not be obeyed—and we do this, not because Congress have no right to pass such laws; this we do not allege;

but because they have passed them with improper views. They are unconstitutional from the motives of those who pass them, which we can never with certainty know, from their unequal operation; although it is impossible from the nature of things that they should be equal—and from the disposition which we presume may be made of their proceeds, although that disposition has not been declared. This is the plain meaning of the ordinance in relation to laws which it abrogates for alleged unconstitutionality. But it does not stop here. It repeals, in express terms, an important part of the Constitution itself, and of laws passed to give it effect, which have never been alleged to be unconstitutional. The Constitution declares that the judicial powers of the United States extend to cases arising under the laws of the United States, and that such laws the Constitution and treaties shall be paramount to the State constitutions and laws. The judiciary act prescribes the mode by which the case may be brought before a court of the United States, by appeal, when a State tribunal shall decide against this provision of the Constitution. The ordinance declares there shall be no appeal; makes the State law paramount to the Constitution and laws of the United States; forces judges and jurors to swear that they will disregard their provisions; and even makes it penal in a suitor to attempt relief by appeal. It further declares that it shall not be lawful for the authorities of the United States, or of that State, to enforce the payment of duties imposed by the revenue laws within its limits.

Here is a law of the United States, not even pretended to be unconstitutional, repealed by the authority of a small majority of the voters of a single State. Here is a provision of the Constitution which is solemnly abrogated by the same authority.

On such expositions and reasonings, the ordinance grounds not only an assertion of the right to annul the laws of which it complains, but to enforce it by a threat of seceding from the Union, if any attempt is made to execute them.

This right to secede is deduced from the nature of the Constitution, which they say is a compact between sovereign States, who have preserved their whole sovereignty, and therefore are subject to no superior; that because they made the compact, they can break it when in their opinion it has been departed from by the other States. Fallacious as this course of reasoning is, it enlists State pride, and finds advocates in the honest prejudices of those who have not studied the nature of our government sufficiently to see the radical error on which it rests.

The people of the United States formed the Constitution, acting through the State legislatures, in making the compact, to meet and discuss its provisions, and acting in separate conventions when they ratified those provisions; but the term used in its construction show it to be a government in which the people of all the States collectively are represented. We are ONE PEOPLE in the choice of the President and Vice-President. Here the States have no other agency than to direct the mode in which the votes shall be given. The candidates having the majority of all the votes are chosen. The electors of a majority of States may have given their votes for one candidate, and yet another may be chosen. The people then, and not the States, are represented in the executive branch.

In the House of Representatives there is this difference, that the people of one State do not, as in the case of President and Vice-President, all vote for all the members, each State electing only its own representatives. But this creates no material distinction. When chosen, they are all representatives of the United States, not representatives of the particular State from which they come. They are paid by the United States, not by the State; nor are they accountable to it for any act done in performance of their legislative functions; and however they may in practice, as it is their duty to do, consult and prefer the interests of their particular constituents when they come in conflict with any other partial or local interest, yet it is their first and highest duty, as representatives of the United States, to promote the general good.

The Constitution of the United States, then, forms a *government*, not a league, and whether it be formed by compact between the States, or in any other manner, its character is the same. It is a government in which all the people are represented, which operates directly on the people individually, not upon the States; they retained all the power they did not grant. But each State having expressly parted with so many powers as to constitute jointly with the other States a single nation, can not from that period possess any right to secede, because such secession does not break a league, but destroys the unity of a nation, and any injury to that unity is not only a breach which would result from the contravention of a compact, but it is an offense against the whole Union. To say that any State may at pleasure secede from the Union, is to say that the United States is not a nation; because it would be a solecism to contend that any part of a nation might dissolve its connection with the other parts, to their injury or ruin, without committing any offense. Secession, like any other revolutionary act, may be morally justified by the extremity of oppression; but to call it a constitutional right, is confounding the meaning of terms, and can only be done through gross error, or to deceive those who are willing to assert a right, but would pause before they made a revolution, or incur the penalties consequent upon a failure.

Because the Union was formed by compact, it is said the parties to that compact may, when they feel aggrieved, depart from it; but it is precisely because it is a compact that they cannot. A contract is an agreement or binding obligation. It may by its terms have a sanction or penalty for its breach, or it may not. If it contains no sanction, it may be broken with no other consequence than moral guilt; if it have a sanction, then the breach incurs the designated or implied penalty. A league between independent nations, generally, has no sanction other than a moral one; or if it should contain a penalty, as there is no common superior, it cannot be enforced. A government, on the contrary, always has a sanction, express or implied; and, in our case, it is both necessarily implied and expressly given. An attempt by force of arms to destroy a government is an offense, by whatever means the constitutional compact may have been formed; and such government has the right, by the law of self-defense, to pass acts for punishing the offender, unless that right is modified, restrained, or resumed by the constitutional act. In our system, although it is modified in the case of treason, yet authority is expressly given to pass all laws necessary to carry its powers into effect, and under this grant provision has been made for punishing acts which obstruct the due administration of the laws.

It would seem superfluous to add anything to show the nature of that union which connects us; but as erroneous opinions on this subject are the foundation of doctrines the most destructive to our peace, I must give some further development to my views on this subject. No one, fellow-citizens, has a higher reverence for the reserved rights of the States than the magistrate who now addresses you. No one would make greater personal sacrifices, or official exertions, to defend them from violation; but equal care must be taken to prevent, on their part, an improper interference with, or resumption of, the rights they have vested in the nation. The line has not been so distinctly drawn as to avoid doubts in some cases of the exercise of power. Men of the best intentions and soundest views may differ in their construction of some parts of the Constitution; but there are others on which dispassionate reflection can leave no doubt. Of this nature appears to be the assumed right of secession. It rests, as we have seen, on the alleged and undivided sovereignty of the States, and of their having formed in this sovereign capacity a compact which is called the Constitution, from which, because they made it, they have the right to secede. Both of these positions are erroneous, and some of the arguments to prove them so have been anticipated.

The States severally have not retained their entire sovereignty. It has been shown that in becoming parts of a nation, not members of a league, they surrendered many of their essential parts of sovereignty. The right to make treaties, declare war, levy taxes, exercise judicial and legislative powers, were all functions of sovereign power. The States, then, for all these important purposes, were no longer sovereign. The allegiance of their citizens was transferred in the first instance to the government of the United States; they became American citizens, and owed obedience to the Constitution of the United States, and to laws made in conformity with the powers vested in Congress. This last position has not been, and can not be, denied. How, then, can that State be said to be sovereign and independent whose citizens owe obedience to laws not made by it, and whose magistrates are sworn to disregard those laws, when they come in conflict with those passed by another? What shows conclusively that the States can not be said to have reserved an undivided sovereignty, is that they expressly ceded the right to punish treason—not treason against a separate power, but treason against the United States. Treason is an offense against *sovereignty*, and sovereignty must reside with the power to punish it. But the reserved rights of the States are not less sacred because they have for their common interest made the general government the depository of these powers. The unity of our political character (as has been shown for another purpose) commenced with its very existence. Under the royal government we had no separate character; our opposition to its oppression began as UNITED COLONIES. We were the UNITED STATES under the Confederation, and the name was perpetuated and the Union rendered more perfect by the federal Constitution. In none of these stages did we consider ourselves in any other light than as forming one nation. Treaties and alliances were made in the name of all. Troops were raised for the joint defense. How, then, with all these proofs, that under all changes of our position we had, for designated purposes and with defined powers, created national governments—how is it that the most perfect of these several modes of union should now be considered as a mere league that may be dissolved at pleasure? It is from an abuse of terms. Compact is used as synonymous with league, although the true term is not employed, because it would at once show the fallacy of the reasoning. It would not do to say that our Constitution was only a league, but it is labored to prove it a compact (which, in one sense, it is), and then to argue that as a league is a compact, every compact between nations must, of course, be a league, and that from such an engagement every sovereign power has a right to recede. But it has been shown that in this sense the States are not sovereign, and that even if they were, and the national Constitution had been formed by compact, there would be no right in any one State to exonerate itself from the obligation.

So obvious are the reasons which forbid this secession, that it is necessary only to allude to them. The Union was formed for the benefit of all. It was produced by mutual sacrifice of interest and opinions. Can those sacrifices be recalled? Can the States, who magnanimously surrendered their title to the territories of the West, recall the grant? Will the inhabitants of the inland States agree to pay the duties that may be imposed without their assent by those on the Atlantic or the Gulf, for their own benefit? Shall there be a free port in one State, and enormous duties in another? No one believes that any right exists in a single State to involve all the others in these and countless other evils, contrary to engagements solemnly made. Every one must see that the other States, in self-defense, must oppose it at all hazards.

These are the alternatives that are presented by the convention: A repeal of all the acts for raising revenue, leaving the government without the means of support; or an acquiesce in the dissolution of our Union by the secession of one of its members. When the first was proposed, it was known that it could not be listened to for a moment. It was known if force was applied to oppose the execution of the laws, that it must be repelled by force—that Congress could not, without involving itself in disgrace and the country in ruin, accede to the proposition; and yet if this is not done in a given day, or if any attempt is made to execute the laws, the State is, by the ordinance, declared to be out of the Union. The majority of a convention assembled for the purpose have dictated these terms, or rather this rejection of all terms, in the name of the people of South Carolina. It is true that the governor of the State speaks of the submission of their grievances to a convention of all the States; which, he says, they "sincerely and anxiously seek and desire." Yet this obvious and constitutional mode of obtaining the sense of the other States on the construction of the federal compact, and amending it, if necessary, has never been attempted by those who have urged the State on to this destructive measure. The State might have proposed a call for a general convention to the other States, and Congress, if a sufficient number of them concurred, must have called it. But the first magistrate of South Carolina, when he expressed a hope that, "on a review by Congress and the functionaries of the general government of the merits of the controversy," such a convention will be accorded to them, must have known that neither Congress, nor any functionary in the general government, has authority to call such a convention, unless it be demanded by two-thirds of the States. This suggestion, then, is another instance of the reckless inattention to the provisions of the Constitution with which this crisis has been madly hurried on; or of the attempt to persuade the people that a constitutional remedy has been sought and refused. If the legislature of South Carolina "anxiously desire" a general convention to consider their complaints, why have they not made application for it in the way the Constitution points out? The assertion that they "earnestly seek" it is completely negatived by the omission.

This, then is the position in which we stand. A small majority of the citizens of one State in the Union have elected delegates to a State convention; that convention has ordained that all the revenue laws of the United States must be repealed, or that they are no longer a member of the Union. The governor of that State has recommended to the legislature the raising of an army to carry the secession into effect, and that he may be empowered to give clearances to vessels in the name of the State. No act of violent opposition to the laws has yet been committed, but such a state of things is hourly apprehended, and it is the intent of this instrument to PROCLAIM, not only that the duty imposed on me by the Constitution, "to take care that the laws be faithfully executed," shall be performed to the extent of the powers already vested in me by law, or of such others as the wisdom of Congress shall devise and intrust to me for that purpose; but to warn the citizens of South Carolina, who have been deluded into an opposition to the laws, of the danger they will incur by obedience to the illegal and disorganizing ordinance of the convention—to exhort those who have refused to support it to persevere in their determination to uphold the Constitution and laws of their country, and to point out to all the perilous situation into which the good people of that State have been led, and that the course they are urged to pursue is one of ruin and disgrace to the very State whose rights they effect to support.

Fellow-citizens of my native State! let me not only admonish you, as the first magistrate of our common country, not to incur the penalty of its laws, but use the influence that a father would over his children whom he saw rushing to a certain ruin. In that paternal language, with that paternal feeling, let me tell you, my countrymen, that you are deluded by men who are either deceived themselves or wish to deceive you. Mark under what pretenses you have been led on to the brink of insurrection and treason on which you stand! First a diminution of the value of our staple commodity, lowered by overproduction in other quarters and the consequent diminution in the value of your lands, were the sole effect of the tariff laws. The effect of those laws was confessedly injurious, but the evil was greatly exaggerated by the unfounded theory you were taught to believe, that its burdens were in proportion to your exports, not to your consumption of imported articles. Your pride was roused by the assertions that a submission to these laws was a state of vassalage, and that resistance to them was equal, in patriotic merit, to the opposition our fathers offered to the oppressive laws of Great Britain. You were told that this opposition might be peaceably—might be constitutionally made—that you might enjoy all the advantages of the Union and bear none of its burdens. Eloquent appeals to your passions, to your State pride, to your native courage, to your sense of real injury, were used to prepare you for the period when the mask which concealed the hideous features of DISUNION should be taken off. It fell, and you were made to look with complacency on objects which not long since you would have regarded with horror. Look back to the arts which have brought you to this state—look forward to the consequences to which it must inevitably lead! Look back to what was first told you as an inducement to enter into this dangerous course. The great political truth was repeated to you that you had the revolutionary right of resisting all laws that were palpably unconstitutional and intolerably oppressive—it was added that the right to nullify a law rested on the same principle, but that it was a peaceable remedy! This character which was given to it, made you receive with too much confidence the assertions that were made of the unconstitutionality of the law and its oppressive effects. Mark, my fellow-citizens, that by the admission of your leaders the unconstitutionality must be *palpable*, or it will justify either resistance or nullification! What is the meaning of the word *palpable* in the sense in which it is here used?—that which is apparent to every one, that which no man of ordinary intellect will fail to perceive. Is the unconstitutionality of these laws of that description? Let those among your leaders who once approved and advocated the principles of protective duties, answer the question; and let them choose whether they will be considered as incapable, then, of perceiving that which must have been apparent to every man of common understanding, or as imposing upon our confidence and endeavoring to mislead you now. In either case, they are unsafe guides in the perilous path they urge you to tread. Ponder well on this circumstance, and you will know how to appreciate the exaggerated language they address to you. They are not champions of liberty emulating the fame of our Revolutionary fathers, nor are you an oppressed people, contending, as they repeat to you, against worse than colonial vassalage. You are free members of a flourishing and happy Union. There is no settled design to oppress you. You have, indeed, felt the unequal operation of laws which may have been unwisely, not unconstitutionally passed; but that inequality must necessarily be removed. At the very moment when you were madly urged on to the unfortunate course you have begun, a change in public opinion has commenced.

The nearly approaching payment of the public debt, and the consequent necessity of a diminution of duties, had already caused a considerable reduction, and that, too, on some articles of general consumption in your State. The importance of this change was underrated, and you were authoritatively told that no further alleviation of your burdens was to be expected, at the very time when the condition of the country imperiously demanded such a modification of the duties as should reduce them to a just and equitable scale. But, as apprehensive of the effect of this change in allaying your discontents, you were precipitated into a fearful state in which you now find yourselves.

I have urged you to look back to the means that were used to hurry you on to the position you have now assumed, and forward to the consequences it will produce. Something more is necessary. Contemplate the condition of that country of which you still form an important part; consider its government uniting in one bond of common interest and general protection so many different States—giving to all their inhabitants the proud title of AMERICAN CITIZENS—protecting their commerce—securing their literature and arts—facilitating their intercommunication—defending their frontiers—and making their name respected in the remotest parts of the earth!

Consider the extent of its territory, its increasing and happy population, its advance in arts, which render life agreeable, and the sciences which elevate the mind! See education spreading the lights of religion, morality, and general information into every cottage in this wide extent of our Territories and States! Behold it as the asylum where the wretched and the oppressed find a refuge and support! Look on this picture of happiness and honor, and say, WE, TOO, ARE CITIZENS OF AMERICA—Carolina is one of these proud States her arms have defended—her best blood has cemented this happy Union! And then add, if you can, without horror and remorse, this happy Union we will dissolve—this picture of peace and prosperity we will deface—this free intercourse we will interrupt—these fertile fields we will deluge with blood—the protection of that glorious flag we renounce—the very name of Americans we discard. And for what, mistaken men! For what do you throw away these inestimable blessings—for what would you exchange your share in the advantages and honor of the Union? For the dream of a separate independence—a dream interrupted by bloody conflicts with your neighbors, and a vile dependence on a foreign power. If your leaders could succeed in establishing a separation, what would be your situation? Are you united at home—are you free from the apprehension of civil discord, with all its fearful consequences? Do our neighboring republics, every day suffering some new revolution or contending with some new insurrection—do they excite your envy? But the dictates of a high duty oblige me solemnly to announce that you can not succeed. The laws of the United States must be executed. I have no discretionary power on the subject—my duty is emphatically pronounced in the Constitution. Those who told you that you might peaceably prevent their execution, deceived you—they could not have been deceived themselves. They know that a forcible opposition could alone prevent the execution of the laws, and they know that such opposition must be repelled. Their object is disunion; but be not deceived by names; disunion, by armed force, is TREASON. Are you really ready to incur this guilt? If you are, on the head of the instigators of the act be the dreadful consequences—on their heads be the dishonor, but on yours may fall the punishment—on your unhappy State will inevitably fall all the evils of the conflict you force upon the government of your country. It cannot accede to the mad project of disunion of which you would be the first victims—its first magistrate can not, if he would, avoid the performance of his duty—the consequence must be fearful for you, distressing to your fellow-citizens here, and to the friends of good government throughout the world. Its enemies have beheld our prosperity with a vexation they could not conceal—it was a standing refutation of their slavish doctrines, and they will point to our discord with the triumph of malignant joy. It is yet in your power to disappoint them. There is yet time to show that the descendants of the Pinckneys, the Sumpters, the Rutledges, and of the thousand other names which adorn the pages of your revolutionary history, will not abandon that Union to support which so many of them fought and bled and died. I adjure you, as you honor their memory—as you love the cause of freedom, to which they dedicated their lives—as you prize the peace of your country, the lives of its best citizens, and your own fair fame, to retrace your steps. Snatch from the archives of your State the disorganizing edict of its convention—bid its members to re-assemble and promulgate the decided expressions of your will to remain in the path which alone can conduct you to safety, prosperity, and honor—tell them that compared to disunion, all other evils are light, because that brings with it an accumulation of all—declare that you will never take the field unless the star-spangled banner of your country shall float over you—that you will not be stigmatized when dead, and dishonored and scorned while you live, as the authors of the first attack on the Constitution of your country!—its destroyers you can not be. You may disturb its peace—you may interrupt the course of its prosperity—you may cloud its reputation for stability—but its tranquillity will be restored, its prosperity will return, and the stain upon its national character will be transferred and remain an eternal blot on the memory of those who caused the disorder.

Fellow-citizens of the United States! the threat of unhallowed disunion—the names of those, once respected, by whom it is uttered—the array of military force to support it—denote the approach of a crisis in our affairs on which the continuance of our unexampled prosperity, our political existence, and perhaps that of all free governments, may depend. The conjecture demanded a free, a full, and explicit enunciation, not only of my intentions, but of my principles of action; and as the claim was asserted of a right by a State to annul the laws of the Union, and even to secede from it at pleasure, a frank exposition of my opinions in relation to the origin and form of our government, and the construction I give to the instrument by which it was created, seemed to be proper. Having the fullest confidence in the justness of the legal and constitutional opinion of my duties which has been expressed, I rely with equal confidence on your undivided support in my determination to execute the laws—to preserve the Union by all constitutional means—to arrest, if possible, by moderate but firm measures, the necessity of a recourse to force; and, if it be the will of Heaven that the recurrence of its primeval curse on man for the shedding of a brother's blood should fall upon our land, that it be not called down by any offensive act on the part of the United States.

Fellow-citizens! the momentous case is before you. On your undivided support of your government depends the decision of the great question it involves, whether your sacred Union will be preserved, and the blessing it secures to us as one people shall be perpetuated. No one can doubt that the unanimity with which that decision will be expressed, will be such as to inspire new confidence in republican institutions, and that the prudence, the wisdom, and the courage which it will bring to their defense, will transmit them unimpaired and invigorated to our children.

May the Great Ruler of nations grant that the signal blessings with which He has favored ours may not, by the madness of party, or personal ambition, be disregarded and lost, and may His wise providence bring those who have produced this crisis to see the folly, before they feel the misery, of civil strife, and inspire a returning veneration for that Union which, if we may dare to penetrate His designs, He has chosen, as the only means of attaining the high destinies to which we may reasonably aspire.

In testimony whereof, I have caused the seal of the United States to be hereunto affixed, having signed the same with my hand.

Done at the City of Washington, this 10th day of December, in the year of our Lord one thousand eight hundred and thirty-two, and of the independence of the United States the fifty-seventh.

ANDREW JACKSON.

By the President.

EDW. LIVINGSOE, *Secretary of State.*

MONROE DOCTRINE.

EXTRACT FROM PRESIDENT MONROE'S ANNUAL MESSAGE, WASHINGTON, DEC. 2, 1823.

THE citizens of the United States cherish sentiments the most friendly in favor of the liberty and happiness of their fellow-men on that side of the Atlantic. In the wars of the European powers, in matters relating to themselves, we have never taken any part, nor does it comport with our policy so to do. It is only when our rights are invaded, or seriously menaced, that we resent injuries or make preparations for our defence. With the movements in this hemisphere, we are, of necessity, more immediately connected, and by causes which must be obvious to all enlightened and impartial observers. The political system of the allied powers is essentially different, in this respect, from that of America. This difference proceeds from that which exists in their respective Governments. And to the defence of our own, which has been achieved by the loss of so much blood and treasure, and matured by the wisdom of their most enlightened citizens, and under which we have enjoyed unexampled felicity, this whole nation is devoted.

We owe it, therefore, to candor and to the amicable relations existing between the United States and those powers, to declare, that we should consider any attempt on their part to extend their system to any portion of this hemisphere, as dangerous to our peace and safety.

With the existing colonies or dependencies of any European power, we have not interfered, and shall not interfere. But, with the Governments who have declared their independence, and maintained it, and whose independence we have, on great consideration, and on just principles, acknowledged, we could not view any interposition for the purpose of oppressing them, or controlling, in any other manner, their destiny, by any European power, in any other light than as the manifestation of an unfriendly disposition towards the United States.

In the war between those new Governments and Spain, we declared our neutrality at the time of their recognition, and to this we have adhered, and shall continue to adhere, provided no change shall occur, which, in the judgment of the competent authorities of this Government, shall make a corresponding change on the part of the United States, indispensable to their security.

THE DRED SCOTT DECISION.

DRED SCOTT, PLAINTIFF IN ERROR, *vs.* JOHN F. A. SANDFORD.

This case was brought up by writ of error, from the Circuit Court of the United States for the district of Missouri.

It was an action of trespass *vi et armis* instituted in the Circuit Court by Scott against Sanford.

Prior to the institution of the present suit, an action was brought by Scott for his freedom in the Circuit Court of St. Louis county, (State court,) where there was a verdict and judgment in his favor. On a writ of error to the Supreme Court of the State, the judgment below was reversed, and the case remanded to the Circuit Court, where it was continued to await the decision of the case now in question.

The declaration of Scott contained three counts: one, that Sandford had assaulted the plaintiff; one, that he had assaulted Harriet Scott, his wife; and one, that he had assaulted Eliza Scott and Lizzie Scott, his children.

Sandford appeared, and filed the following plea:

DRED SCOTT,
vs.
JOHN F. A. SANDFORD. } *Plea to the Jurisdiction of the Court.*

APRIL TERM, 1854.

And the said John F. A. Sandford, in his own proper person, comes and says that this court ought not to have or take further cognizance of the action aforesaid, because he says that said cause of action, and each and every of them, (if any such have accrued to the said Dred Scott,) accrued to the said Dred Scott out of the jurisdiction of this court, and exclusively within the jurisdiction of the courts of the State of Missouri, for that, to wit: the said plaintiff, Dred Scott, is not a citizen of the State of Missouri, as alleged in his declaration, because he is a negro of African descent; his ancestors were of pure African blood, and were brought into this country and sold as negro slaves, and this the said Sandford is ready to verify. Wherefore he prays judgment whether this court can or will take further cognizance of the action aforesaid.

JOHN F. A. SANDFORD.

To this plea there was a demurrer in the usual form, which was argued in April, 1854, when the court gave judgment that the demurrer should be sustained.

In May, 1854, the defendant, in pursuance of an agreement between counsel, and with the leave of the court, pleaded in bar of the action:

1. Not guilty.

2. That the plaintiff was a negro slave, the lawful property of the defendant, and, as such, the defendant gently laid his hands upon him, and thereby had only restrained him, as the defendant had a right to do.

3. That with respect to the wife and daughters of the plaintiff, in the second and third counts of the declaration mentioned, the defendant had, as to them, only acted in the same manner, and in virtue of the same legal right.

In the first of these pleas, the plaintiff joined issue; and to the second and third filed replications alleging that the defendant, of his own wrong and without the cause in his second and third pleas alleged, committed the trespasses, etc.

The counsel then filed the following agreed statement of facts, viz.:

In the year 1834, the plaintiff was a negro slave belonging to Dr. Emerson, who was a surgeon in the army of the United States. In that year, 1834, said Dr. Emerson took the plaintiff from the State of Missouri to the military post at Rock Island in the State of Illinois, and held him there as a slave until the month of April or May, 1836. At the time last mentioned, said Dr. Emerson removed the plantiff from said military post at Rock Island to the military post at Fort Snelling, situate on the west bank of the Mississippi river. in the Territory known as Upper Louisiana, acquired by the United States of France, and situate north of the latitude of thirty-six degrees thirty minutes north, and north of the State of Missouri. Said Dr. Emerson held the plaintiff in slavery at said Fort Snelling, from said last-mentioned date until the year 1838.

In the year 1835, Harriet, who is named in the second count of the plaintiff's declaration, was the negro slave of Major Taliaferro, who belonged to the army of the United States. In that year, 1835, said Major Taliaferro took said Harriet to said Fort Snelling, a military post, situated as hereinbefore stated, and kept her there as a slave until the year 1836, and then sold and delivered her as a slave at said Fort Snelling unto the said Dr. Emerson hereinbefore named. Said Dr. Emerson held said Harriet in slavery at said Fort Snelling until the year 1838.

In the year 1836, the plaintiff and said Harriet, at said Fort Snelling, with the consent of said Dr. Emerson, who then claimed to be their master and owner, intermarried, and took each other for husband and wife. Eliza and Lizzie, named in the third count of the plaintiff's declaration, are the fruit of that marriage. Eliza is about fourteen years old, and was born on board the steamboat Gipsey, north of the north line of the State of Missouri, and upon the river Mississippi. Lizzie is about seven years old, and was born in the State of Missouri, at the military post called Jefferson Barracks.

In the year 1838, said Dr. Emerson removed the plaintiff and said Harriet and their said daughter Eliza, from said Fort Snelling to the State of Missouri, where they have ever since resided.

Before the commencement of this suit, said Dr. Emerson sold and conveyed the plaintiff, said Harriet, Eliza, and Lizzie, to the defendant, as slaves, and the defendant has ever since claimed to hold them and each of them as slaves.

At the times mentioned in the plaintiff's declaration, the defendant claiming to be owner as aforesaid, laid his hands upon said plaintiff, Harriet, Eliza, and Lizzie, and imprisoned them, doing in this respect, however, no more than what he might lawfully do if they were of right his slaves at such times.

Further proof may be given on the trial for either party.

It is agreed that Dred Scott brought suit for his freedom in the Circuit Court of St. Louis county; that there was a verdict and judgment in his favor; that on a writ of error to the Supreme Court, the judgment below was reversed, and the same remanded to the Circuit Court, where it has been continued to await the decision of this case.

In May, 1854, the cause went before a jury, who found the following verdict, viz.: "As to the first issue joined in this case, we of the jury find the defendant not guilty; and as to the issue secondly above joined, we of the jury find that before and at the time when, &c., in the first count mentioned, the said Dred Scott was a negro slave, the lawful property of the defendant; and as to the issue thirdly above joined, we, the jury, find that before and at the time when, &c., in the second and third counts mentioned, the said Harriet, wife of said Dred Scott, and Eliza and Lizzie, the daughters of the said Dred Scott, were negro slaves, the lawful property of the defendant."

Whereupon the court gave judgment for the defendant.

After an ineffectual motion for a new trial, the plaintiff filed the following bill of exceptions.

On the trial of this cause by the jury, the plaintiff, to maintain the issues on his part, read to the jury the following agreed statment of facts, (see agreement above.) No further testimony was given to the jury by either party. Thereupon the plaintiff moved the court to give to the jury the following instruction, viz.:

"That upon the facts agreed to by the parties, they ought to find for the plaintiff. The court refused to give such instruction to the jury, and the plaintiff, to such refusal, then and there duly excepted."

The court then gave the following instruction to the jury, on motion of the defendant:

"The jury are instructed, that upon the facts in this case, the law is with the defendant." The plaintiff excepted to this instruction.

Upon these exceptions, the case came up to this court.

It was argued at December term, 1855, and ordered to be reargued at the present term.

The opinion of the court, as delivered by Chief Justice Taney, being so lengthy, we omit all but the summing up, to wit:

Upon the whole, therefore, it is the judgment of this court, that it appears by the record before us, that the plaintiff in error is not a citizen of Missouri, in the sense in which that word is used in the Constitution; and that the Circuit Court of the United States, for that reason, had no jurisdiction in the case, and could give no judgment in it. Its judgment for the defendant must, consequently, be reversed, and a mandate issued, directing the suit to be dismissed for want of jurisdiction.

PRESIDENTS AND VICE-PRESIDENTS OF THE UNITED STATES.

WITH THE VOTE FOR EACH CANDIDATE FOR OFFICE.

BEFORE THE REVOLUTION.

First Congress, Sept. 5, 1774. Peyton Randolph, of Virginia, President. Born in Virginia, in 1723, died at Philadelphia, Oct. 22, 1785. Charles Thomson, of Pennsylvania, Secretary. Born in Ireland, 1730, died in Pennsylvania, Aug. 16, 1824.

Second Congress, May 10, 1775. Peyton Randolph, President. Resigned May 24, 1775.

John Hancock, of Massachusetts, elected his successor. He was born at Quincy, Mass., 1737, died Oct. 8, 1793. He was President of Congress until October, 1777.

Henry Laurens, of South Carolina, President from Nov. 1, 1777, to Dec. 1778. He was born at Charleston, S. C., 1724, died in South Carolina, Dec., 1792.

John Jay, of New York, President from Dec. 10,

1778, to Sept. 27, 1779. He was born in New York City, Dec. 12, 1745, died at New York, May 17, 1829.

Samuel Huntingdon, of Connecticut, President from Sept. 28, 1779, until July 10, 1781. He was born in Connecticut, in 1732, died 1796.

Thos. McKean, of Pennsylvania, President from July 1781, until Nov. 5, 1781. He was born in Pennsylvania, March 19, 1734, died at Philadelphia, June 24, 1817.

John Hanson, of Maryland, President from Nov. 5, 1781, to Nov. 4, 1782.

Elias Boudinot, of New Jersey, President from Nov. 4, 1782, until Feb. 4, 1783. He was born at Philadelphia, May 2, 1740, died 1824.

Thomas Mifflin, of Pennsylvania, President from Feb. 4, 1783, to Nov. 30, 1784. Born at Philadelphia, 1744, died in the same city, Jan. 21, 1800.

Richard Henry Lee, of Virginia, President from Nov. 30, 1784, to Nov. 23, 1785. He was born in Virginia, 1732, died 1794.

John Hancock, of Massachusetts, President from Nov. 23, 1785, to June 6, 1786.

Nathaniel Gorham, of Massachusetts, President from June 6, 1786, to Feb. 2, 1787. He was born at Charlestown, Mass., 1738, died June 11, 1796.

Arthur St. Clair, of Pennsylvania, President from Feb. 2, 1787, to Jan. 28, 1788. He was born in Edinburgh, Scotland, ——, died in 1818.

Cyrus Griffin, of Virginia, President from Jan. 28, 1788, to the end of the Congress under the

Confederation, March 3, 1789. He was born in England, 1748, died in Virginia, 1810.

UNDER THE CONSTITUTION.

1789 to 1793.—George Washington, of Virginia, inaugurated as President of the United States, April 30, 1789. He was born upon Wakefield estate, Virginia, Feb. 22, (11th old style,) 1732, died at Mount Vernon, Dec. 14, 1799.

John Adams, of Massachusetts, Vice-President. Born at Braintree, Mass., Oct. 19, 1735, died July 4, 1826, near Quincy, Mass.

Electoral vote.—Geo. Washington, 69; John Adams, 34; John Jay, New York, 9; R. H. Harrison, Maryland, 6; John Rutledge, South Carolina, 6; John Hancock, Massachusetts, 4; Geo. Clinton, New York, 3; Sam'l Huntingdon, Connecticut, 2; John Milton, Georgia, 2; James Armstrong, Georgia, 1; Edward Telfair, Georgia, 1; Benj. Lincoln, Massachusetts, 1—Total, 69. Ten States voted,—Rhode Island, New York, and North Carolina not voting, not having ratified the Constitution in time.

1793 to 1797.—George Washington, President, inaugurated March 4, 1793.

John Adams, Vice-President.

Electoral vote.—Geo. Washington, 132; John Adams, 77; Geo. Clinton, 50; Thos. Jefferson, Virgia, 4; Aaron Burr, New York, 1.—Total, 132. Fifteen States voted.

1797 to 1801.—John, Adams President, inaugurated March 4, 1797.

Thomas Jefferson, of Virginia, Vice-President. Born at Shadwell, Virginia, April 13, 1743, died at Monticello, Virginia, July 4, 1826.

Electoral vote.—John Adams, 71; Thomas Jefferson, 68; Thomas Pinckney, South Carolina, 59; Aaron Burr, 30; Sam'l Adams, Massachusetts, 15; Oliver Ellsworth, Connecticut, 11; Geo. Clinton, 7; John Jay, 5; James Iredell, North Carolina, 3; George Washington, 2; John Henry, Maryland, 2; S. Johnson, North Carolina, 2; Charles C. Pinckney, South Carolina, 1.—Total 138. Sixteen States voting.

1801 to 1805.—Thomas Jefferson, President, inaugurated March 4, 1801.

Aaron Burr, of New York Vice-President. Born at Newark, N. J., Feb. 6, 1756, died at Staten Island, N. Y., Sept. 14, 1836.

Electoral vote.—Thos. Jefferson, 73; Aaron Burr, 73; John Adams, 65; Chas. C. Pinckney, 64; John Jay 1.—Total, 13. Sixteen States voting.

There was no choice by the Electoral colleges, and the election was carried into the House of Representatives, and upon the 36th ballot, ten States voted for Jefferson, four States for Aaron Burr, and two States in blank. Jefferson was declared to be elected President, and Burr Vice-President. The Constitution was then amended, so that the Vice-President was voted for separately, instead of being the second on the vote for President.

1805 to 1809.—Thomas Jefferson, President, inaugurated March 4, 1805.

George Clinton, of New York, Vice-President. He was born in Ulster county, N. Y., 1739, died in Washington, D. C., April 20, 1812.

ELECTORAL VOTE.—For President, Thos. Jefferson, 162; Chas. Cotesworth Pinckney, 14.—Total, 176. Seven States voting. For Vice-President, George Clinton, 162; Rufus King, New York, 14.

1809 to 1813.—James Madison, of Virginia, President, inaugurated March 4, 1809. He was born March 16, 1751, in Prince George county, Va., and died at Montpelier, Va., June 28, 1836.

George Clinton, of New York, Vice-President, until his death, April 20, 1812.

ELECTORAL VOTE.—For President, James Madison, 122; Geo. Clinton, 6; C. C. Pinckney, 47.—Total, 175. Seventeen States voting. For Vice-President, George Clinton, 113; James Madison, 3; James Monroe, Virginia, 3; John Langdon, New Hampshire, 9; Rufus King, New York, 47.

1813 to 1817.—James Madison, of Virginia, President, inaugurated March 4, 1813.

Elbridge Gerry, of Massachusetts, Vice-President, until his death, Nov. 23, 1814. He was born at Marblehead, Mass., July 17, 1744, and died at Washington, D. C.

ELECTORAL VOTE.—For President, James Madison, 128; De Witt Clinton, New York, 89.—Total, 217. Eighteen States voting. For Vice-President, Elbridge Gerry, 131; Jared Ingersoll, Pa., 86.

1817 to 1821.—James Monroe, of Virginia, President, inaugurated March 4, 1817. He was born in Westmoreland county, Va., 1759, and died in New York, July 4, 1831.

Daniel D. Tompkins, of New York, Vice-President. Born June 21, 1774, at Fox Meadows, N. Y., and died at Staten Island, June 11, 1825.

Electoral vote.—For President, James Monroe, 183; Rufus King, 34.—Total, 221. Nineteen States voting. For Vice-President, Daniel D. Tompkins, 183; John Eager Howard, Maryland, 22; James Ross, Pennsylvania, 5; John Marshall, Virginia, 4; Robt. Goodloe Harper, Maryland, 3.

1821 to 1825.—James Monroe, President, inaugurated March 4, 1821.

Daniel D. Tompkins, Vice-President.

Electoral vote.—For President, James Monroe, 231; John Quincy Adams, Massachusetts, 1.—Total, 232. Twenty-four States voting. For Vice-President, Daniel D. Tompkins, 218; Richard Stockton, New Jersey, 8; Robert G. Harper, 1; Richard Rush, Pennsylvania, 1; Daniel Rodney, Delaware, 1.

1825 to 1829.—John Quincy Adams, of Massachusetts, President, inaugurated March 4, 1825. He was born at Quincy, Massachusetts, July 11, 1767, and died at Washington City, Feb. 23, 1848.

John Caldwell Calhoun, of South Carolina, Vice-President. Born in Abbeville district, S. C., March 18, 1782, and died March 31, 1850, in Washington City.

Popular vote.—For President, John Quincy

Adams, 105,321; Andrew Jackson, Tennessee, 152,899; Wm. H. Crawford, Georgia, 47,265; Henry Clay, Kentucky, 47,087.

ELECTORAL VOTE.—For President Andrew Jackson, 99; John Quincy Adams, 84; Wm. H. Crawford, 41; Henry Clay, 37.—Total, 261. Twenty-four States voting.

There being no choice by the Electoral colleges, the vote was taken into the House of Representatives. Adams received the votes of thirteen States, Jackson seven, and Crawford four. John Quincy Adams was therefore declared elected President.

For Vice-President, the Electoral vote was John C. Calhoun, South Carolina, 182; Nathan Sanford, New York, 30; Nathaniel Macon, Georgia, 24; Andrew Jackson, Tennessee, 13; Martin Van Buren, New York, 9; Henry Clay, Kentucky, 2.

1829 to 1833.—Andrew Jackson, of Tennessee, President, inaugurated March 4, 1829. He was born in Mecklenburg county, N. C., March 15, 1767, and died at the Hermitage, Tenn., June 8, 1845.

John Caldwell Calhoun, Vice-President, until his resignation, Dec. 28, 1832.

POPULAR VOTE.—For President, Andrew Jackson, 650,028; John Quincy Adams, 512,158.

ELECTORAL VOTE.—For President, Andrew Jackson, 178; J. Q. Adams, 83.—Total, 261. Twenty-four States voting.

For Vice-President, John C. Calhoun, 171; Richard Rush, Pennsylvania, 83; Wm. Smith, South Carolina, 7.

1833 to 1837.– Andrew Jackson, President, inaugurated March 4, 1833.

Martin Van Buren, of New York, Vice-President. He was born at Kinderhook, N. Y., Dec. 5, 1782.

Popular vote.—For President, Andrew Jackson, 687,502; Henry Clay, 550,189; Opposition, (John Floyd, Virginia, and Wm. Wirt, Maryland,) 33,108.

Electoral vote.—For President, Andrew Jackson, 219; Henry Clay, 49; John Floyd, 11; Wm. Wirt, 7.—Total 288. Twenty-four States voting.

For Vice-President, Martin Van Buren, 189; John Sergeant, Pennsylvania, 49; William Wilkins, Pennsylvania, 30; Henry Lee, Massachusetts, 11; Amos Ellmaker, Pennsylvania, 7.

1837 to 1841.—Martin Van Buren, President, inaugurated March 4, 1837.

Richard M. Johnson, of Kentucky, Vice-President. He was born in 1780, and died Nov. 19, 1850.

Popular vote.—For President, Martin Van Buren, 762,149; Opposition, (Wm. H. Harrison, Hugh L. White, Daniel Webster, W. P. Mangum,) 736,736.

Electoral vote.—For President, Martin Van Buren, 170; Wm. H. Harrison, Ohio, 73; Hugh L. White, Tennessee, 26; Daniel Webster, Massachusetts, 14; W. P. Mangum, 11.—Total, 294. Twenty-six States voting.

For Vice-President, Richard M. Johnson, Kentucky, 147; Francis Granger, New York, 77; John Tyler, Virginia, 47; Wm. Smith, Alabama, 23.

1841 to 1845—Wm. Henry Harrison, of Ohio, President, until his death, at Washington, April 4, 1841. He was inaugurated March 4, 1841. He was born in Berkeley county, Va., Feb. 9, 1773.

John Tyler, of Virginia, Vice-President. He was born April, 1790, at Greenway, Charles City county, Va.

John Tyler, of Virginia, became President by the death of W. H. Harrison. He took the oath of office April 6, 1841.

Popular vote—Nov. 1840.—For President, Wm. Henry Harrison, 1,274,783; Martin Van Buren, 1,128,702; James G. Birney, New York, (Abolition,) 7,609.

Electoral vote.—For President, W. H. Harrison, 234; M. Van Buren, 60.—Total, 294. Twenty-six States voting.

For Vice-President, John Tyler, 234; Richard M. Johnson, 48; L. W. Tazewell, South Carolina, 11; James K. Polk, Tennessee, 1.

1845 to 1849.—James Knox Polk, of Tennessee, President, inaugurated March 4, 1845. He was born in Mecklenburg county, North Carolina, Nov. 2, 1795, and died at Nashville, Tennessee, June 15, 1849.

George Mifflin Dallas, of Pennsylvania, Vice-President. Born in Philadelphia, July 10, 1792.

Popular vote.—For President, James K. Polk, 1,335,834; Henry Clay, 1,297,033; James G. Birney, 62,290.

Electoral vote.—For President, James K. Polk,

170; Henry Clay, 105.—Total, 275. Twenty-six States voting.

For Vice-President, George M. Dallas, 170; Theodore Frelinghuysen, of New Jersey, 105.

1849 to 1853.—Zachary Taylor, of Louisiana, President, inaugurated March 4, 1849. Born in Virginia, 1784, died in Washington City, July 9, 1850.

Millard Fillmore, of New York, Vice-President. Born in Locke township, Cayuga county, N. Y., Jan. 7, 1800.

Millard Fillmore, President, after the death of Zachary Taylor, July 9, 1850. He took the oath of office, July 10, 1850.

Popular vote.—For President, Zachary Taylor, 1,362,031; Lewis Cass, of Michigan, 1,222,445; Martin Van Buren, (Free-Soil,) 291,455.

Electoral vote.—For President, Zachary Taylor, 163; Lewis Cass, 127.—Total, 290. Thirty States voting.

For Vice-President, Millard Fillmore, 163; William O. Butler, Kentucky, 127.

1853 to 1857.—Franklin Pierce, of New Hampshire, President, inaugurated March 5, 1853. He was born at Hillsboro, N. H., Nov. 23, 1804.

William R. King, of Alabama, Vice-President. He was born in North Carolina, April 7, 1786, died at Cahawba, Ala., April 18, 1853.

Popular vote.—For President, Franklin Pierce, 1,590,490; Winfield Scott, 1,378,589; John P. Hale, New Hampshire, (Abolition,) 157,296.

Electoral vote.—For President, Franklin Pierce, 254; Winfield Scott of New Jersey, 42.—Total, 296. Thirty-one States voting.

For Vice President, Wm. R. King, 254; Wm. A. Graham, North Carolina, 42.

1857 to 1861.—James Buchanan, of Pennsylvania, President. He was born at Stony Batter, Franklin county, Penn., April 22, 1791.

John C. Breckenridge, of Kentucky, Vice-President. Born near Lexington, Kentucky, Jan. 21, 1820.

Popular vote.—For President, James Buchanan, (Democratic.) 1,832,232; John C. Fremont, California, (Republican,) 1,341,514; Millard Fillmore, New York, (American,) 874,707.

Electoral vote.—For President, James Buchanan, 174; John C. Fremont, 109; Millard Fillmore, 8.—Total, 291. Thirty-one States voting.

For Vice-President, John Breckenridge, 174; Wm. L. Dayton, New Jersey, 109; A. J. Donelson, Tennessee, 8.—Total, 291.

1861 to 1865.—Abraham Lincoln, of Illinois, President, inaugurated March 4, 1861. He was born near Muldraugh's Hill, Hardin county, Ky., Feb. 1809.

Hannibal Hamlin, of Maine, Vice-President. He was born at Paris, Oxford county, Me., Aug. 27, 1809.

Popular vote.—For President, Abraham Lincoln, (Republican,) 1,857,610; Stephen A. Douglas, of Illinois, (Democratic,) 1,365,976; John C. Breckenridge, of Kentucky, (Democratic,) 847,953; John Bell, of Tennessee, (Constitutional Union,) 590,631.

ELECTORAL VOTE.—For President, Abraham Lincoln, 180; John C. Breckinridge, 72; John Bell, 39; Stephen A. Douglas, 12.—Total, 291. Thirty-three States voting.

For Vice-President, Hannibal Hamlin, Maine, 180; Joseph Lane, Oregon, 72; Edward Everett, Massachusetts, 39; Herschel V. Johnson, Georgia, 12.

1865 to 1869.—Abraham Lincoln, President, inaugurated March 4, 1865.

Andrew Johnson, of Tennessee, Vice-President.

POPULAR VOTE.—For President, Abraham Lincoln, (Republican,) 3,213,035; George B. McClellan, (Democrat,) 1,811,754.

Upon the assassination of President Lincoln, April 14, 1865, Andrew Johnson, then Vice-President, assumed the Presideney, and Lafayette S. Foster, of Norwich, Conn., President of the Senate, became Vice-President.

POPULAR NAMES OF STATES.

Virginia, the Old Dominion.
Massachusetts, the Bay State.
Maine, the Border State.
Rhode Island, Little Rhody.
New York, the Empire State.
New Hampshire, the Granite State.
Vermont, the Green Mountain State.
Connecticut, the Land of Steady Habits.
Pennsylvania, the Keystone State.
North Carolina, the Old North State.
Ohio, the Buckeye State.
South Carolina, the Palmetto State.
Michigan, the Wolverine State.
Kentucky, the Corn-Cracker.
Delaware, the Blue Hen's Chicken.
Missouri, the Puke State.
Indiana, the Hoosier State.
Illinois, the Sucker State.
Iowa, the Hawkeye State.
Wisconsin, the Badger State.
Florida, the Peninsular State.
Texas, the Lone Star State.

BATTLES OF THE REVOLUTION.

The following statistics show the losses of life in the various battles of the American Revolution, also the dates of the several battles:

	British Loss.	American Loss.
Lexington, April 15, 1775	273	84
Bunker Hill, June 17, 1775	1054	456
Flatbush, August 12, 1776	400	200
White Plains, August 26, 1776	400	400
Trenton, December 25, 1776	1000	9
Princeton, January 5, 1777	400	100
Hubbardstown, August 17, 1777	800	800
Bennington, August 16, 1777	800	100
Brandywine, September 11, 1777	500	1100
Stillwater, September 17, 1777	600	350
Germantown, October 5, 1777	600	1250
Saratoga, October 17, 1777*	5752	....
Red Hook, October 22, 1777	500	32
Monmouth, June 25, 1778	400	130
Rhode Island, August 27, 1778	260	214
Briar Creek, March 30, 1779	13	400
Stony Point, July 15, 1779	600	100
Camden, August 16, 1779	375	610
King's Mountain, October 1, 1780	950	66
Cowpens, January 17, 1781	800	72
Guilford C. H., March 15, 1781	532	400
Hobkirk's Hill, April 25, 1781	400	460
Eutaw Springs, September, 1781	1000	550
Yorktown, October, 1781*	7072	....
Total	25,481	7913

* Surrendered.

NEUTRALITY LAW OF THE UNITED STATES,

AS AMENDED AND APPROVED BY CONGRESS, JULY 26, 1866.

A Bill more effectually to preserve the neutral relations of the United States.

Be it enacted, &c., That if any citizen of the United States shall, within the territory or jurisdiction thereof, accept and exercise a commission to serve a foreign prince, State, colony, district, or people in war by land or by sea against any prince, State, colony, district or people with whom the United States are at peace, the person so offending shall be deemed guilty of a misdemeanor, and shall on conviction thereof be punished by a fine of not exceeding $2,000 and imprisonment not exceeding two years, or either, at the discretion of the Court in which such offender may be convicted.

SEC. 2. *And be it further enacted*, That if any

person shall, within the territory or jurisdiction of the United States enlist, or enter himself, or hire or retain another person to enlist or enter himself, or to go beyond the limits or jurisdiction of the United States, with intent to be enlisted or entered into the service of any foreign prince, State, colony, district or people as a soldier, or as a marine or seaman on board of any vessel-of-war, letter-of-marque or privateer, every person so offending shall be deemed guilty of a misdemeanor, and shall upon conviction therefor be punished by fine not exceeding $1,000, and imprisonment not exceeding two years, or either of them, at the discretion of the Court, in case such offender shall be convicted; provided that this act shall not be construed to extend to any subject or citizen of any foreign prince, State, colony, district or people, who shall transiently be within the United States, and shall be on board of any vessel of war, letter-of-marque or privateer, which, at the time of its arrival within the United States, was fitted and equipped as such, enlist or enter himself, and hire or retain another subject or citizen of the same foreign prince, State, colony, district or people, who is transiently in the United States, to enlist or enter himself to serve such foreign prince, State, colony, district or people, on board such vessel of war, letter-of-marque or privateer, if the United States shall then be at peace with such foreign prince, State, colony, district or people.

SEC. 3. *And be it further enacted*, That if any person shall within the limits of the United States fit out and arm or attempt to fit out and arm, or procure to be fitted out and armed, or shall knowingly be concerned in the furnishing, fitting out and arming of any ship or vessel with intent that such ship or vessel shall be employed in the service of any foreign prince, State, colony, district or people, to cruise or commit hostilities against the subjects, citizens or property of any foreign prince, State, or any colony, district or people with whom the United States are at peace, or shall issue or deliver a commission within the territory or jurisdiction of the United States for any ship or vessel to the intent that she may be employed as aforesaid, or shall have on board any person or persons who shall have been enlisted, or shall have engaged to enlist or serve or shall be departing from the jurisdiction of the United States with intent to enlist or serve in contravention of the provisions of this act, every person so offending shall be deemed guilty of a misdemeanor, and shall, upon conviction thereof, be punished by a fine not exceeding $3,000, and imprisonment not exceeding three years, or either of them, at the discretion of the Court in which such offender shall be convicted; and every such ship and vessel, with her tackle, apparel and furniture, together with all materials, arms, ammunition and stores which may have been procured for the building and equipment thereof, shall be forfeited to the United States of America.

SEC. 4. *And be it further enacted*, That it shall be lawful for any Collector of the Customs who is by law empowered to make seizures for any forfeiture incurred under any of the laws of Customs, to seize such ships and vessels in such places and in such manner in which the officers of the Customs are empowered to make seizures under the law for the collection and protection of the revenue, and that every such ship and vessel, with the tackle, apparel and furture, together with all the materials, arms, ammunition and stores which may belong to or be on board such ship or vessel, may be prosecuted or condemned for the violation of the provisions of this act in like manner as ships or vessels may be prosecuted and condemned for any breach of the laws made for the collection and protection of the revenue.

SEC. 5. *And be it further enacted*, That if any person shall within the territory or jurisdiction of the United States, increase or augment, or procure to be increased or augmented, or shall knowingly be concerned in increasing or augmenting the force of any ship of war, or cruiser, or other armed vessel, which at the time of her arrival within the United States was a ship of war, or cruiser, or armed vessel in the service of any foreign prince, State, colony, district or people, or belonged to the subjects or citizens of any such prince, State, colony, district or people, the same being at war with any foreign prince, State, colony, district or people with whom the United States are at peace, by adding to the number of guns of such vessel, or by changing those on board of her for guns of a larger calibre, or by addition thereto of any equipment solely applicable to war, or shall have on board any person or persons who shall have enlisted, or engaged to enlist or serve, or who shall be departing from the jurisdiction of the United States with intent to enlist or serve in contravention of the provisions of this act; every person so offending shall be deemed guilty of a misdemeanor, and shall upon conviction thereof be punished by fine or imprisonment, or either of them, at the discretion of the court in which such offender shall be convicted.

SEC. 6. *And be it further enacted*, That the District Courts shall take cognizance of all complaints, informations, indictments, or other prosecutions, by whomsoever instituted, in cases of captures made within the waters of the United States or within a marine league of the coasts or shores thereof.

SEC. 7. *And be it further enacted*, That in every

case in which a vessel shall be fitted out and armed, or in which the force of any vessel of war, cruiser, or other armed vessel shall be increased or augmented, in every case of the capture of a ship or vessel within the jurisdiction or protection of the United States, as before defined, and in every case in which any process issuing out of any court of the United States shall be disobeyed or resisted by any person or persons having the custody of any vessel of war, cruiser or other armed vessel of any prince or State, or of any colony, district or people, or of any subjects or citizens of any foreign prince, State, or of any colony, district or people in any such case, it shall be lawful for the President of the United States, or such other person as he shall have empowered for that purpose to employ such part of the land and naval forces of the United States or of the militia thereof, for the purpose of taking of and detaining any such ship or vessel with her prize or prizes, if any, in order to the execution of the prohibition or penalties of this act, and to the restoring the prize or prizes in the cases in which restoration shall have been adjudged.

SEC. 8. *And be it futher enacted*, That it shall be lawful for the President of the United States, or such person as he shall empower for that purpose, to employ such part of the land and naval forces of the United States, or of the militia thereof, as shall be necessary to compel any foreign ship or vessel to depart the United States in all cases in which, by the laws of nations or the treaties of the United States they ought not to remain within the United States.

SEC. 9. *And be it further enacted*, That offences made punishable by the provisions of this act, committed by citizens of the United States, beyond the jurisdiction of the Uuited States, may be prosecuted and tried before any court having jurisdiction of the offences prohibited by this act.

SEC. 10. *And be it further enacted*, That nothing in this act shall be so construed as to prohibit citizens of the United States from selling vessels, ships or steamers built within the limits thereof, or materials or munitions of war, the growth or product of the same, to inhabitants of other countries, or to Governments not at war with the United States: provided that the operation of this section of this act shall be suspended by the President of the United States with regard to any classes of purchases, whenever the United States shall be engaged in war, or whenever the maintenance of friendly relations with any foreign nation may in his judgment require it.

SEC. 11. *And be it further enacted*, That nothing in the foregoing act shall be construed to prevent the prosecution or punishment of treason, or any piracy or other felony defined by the laws of the United States.

SEC. 12. *And be it further enacted*, That all acts and parts of acts inconsistent with the provisions of this act or inflicting any further or other penalty or forfeiture than are hereinbefore provided for. The acts forbidden herein are hereby repealed.

POPULATION OF THE UNITED STATES.

STATES.	1850.	1860.
Alabama	771,623	964,296
Arkansas	209,897	435,427
California	92,597	380,015
Connecticut	370,792	460,151
Delaware	91,532	112,218
Florida	87,445	140,439
Georgia	906,185	1,057,327
Illinois	851,470	1,711,753
Indiana	988,416	1,350,479
Iowa	192,214	674,948
Kansas	......	107,710
Kentucky	982,405	1,155,713
Louisiana	517,762	709,433
Maine	583,169	628,276
Maryland	583,034	687,034
Massachusetts	994,514	1,231,065
Michigan	397,654	749,112
Minnesota	6,077	162,022
Mississipi	606,026	791,395
Missouri	682,044	1,173,317
New Hampshire	317,976	326,072
New Jersey	489,555	672,031
New York	3,097,394	3,887,542
North Carolina	869,039	992,667
Ohio	1,980,329	2,339,599

STATES.	1850.	1860.
Oregon	12,093	52,464
Pennsylvania	2,311,786	2,906,370
Rhode Island	147,545	174,621
South Carolina	668,507	703,812
Tennessee	1,002,717	1,109,847
Texas	212,592	601,039
Vermont	314,120	315,116
Virginia	1,421,661	1,596,083
Wisconsin	305,391	775,873
TERRITORIES, ETC.		
Colorado	....	34,197
Dakotah	....	4,839
Nebraska	....	28,842
Nevada	... ...	6,857
New Mexico	61,547	93,541
Utah	11,380	40,295
Washington	1,201	11,578
District of Columbia	51,687	75,076
Total	23,191,876	31,429,891

SLAVE POPULATION IN THE U. S. IN 1860.

STATES.	1850.	1860.
Alabama	342,844	435,132
Arkansas	47,100	111,104
Delaware	2,290	1,798
Florida	39,310	61,753
Georgia	381,682	462,230
Kentucky	210,981	225,490
Louisiana	244,809	332,520
Maryland	90,368	87,188
Mississippi	309,878	436,696
Missouri	87,422	114,965

STATES.	1850.	1860.
North Carolina..............	288,548	331,081
South Carolina..............	384,984	402,541
Tennessee..................	239,459	275,784
Texas.......................	58,161	180.388
Virginia.....................	472,528	490,887
Nebraska (Territory)........	..	10
Utah "	..	29
New Mexico "	26	24
District of Columbia.........	3,687	3,181
Total........	3,204,077	3,952,801

STATISTICS OF SLAVERY BEFORE THE REVOLUTION.

AMERICAN SLAVERY IN 1715.

In the reign of George I., the ascertained population of the Continental Colonies was as follows :

	White Men.	Negro Slaves.
New Hampshire...............	9,500	150
Massachusetts..................	94,000	2,000
Rhode Island..................	7,500	500
Connecticut	46,000	1,500
New York......................	27,000	4,000
Pennsylvania	43,300	2,500
New Jersey....................	21,000	1,500
Maryland.......................	40,700	9,400
Virginia.........................	72,000	23,000
North Carolina..................	7,500	3,700
South Carolina..................	6,250	10,500
Total..................	375,000	58,550

SPEECH OF HON. STEPHEN A. DOUGLAS.

DELIVERED AT CHICAGO, MAY 1ST, 1861.

MR. CHAIRMAN: I thank you for the kind terms in which you have been pleased to welcome me. I thank the Committee and citizens of Chicago for this grand and imposing reception. I beg you to believe that I will not do you nor myself the injustice to believe this magnificent ovation is personal homage to myself. I rejoice to know that it expresses your devotion to the Constitution, the Union, and the flag of our country. (Cheers.)

I will not conceal gratification at the uncontrovertible test this vast audience presents—that what political differences or party questions may have divided us, yet you all had a conviction that when the country should be in danger, my loyalty could be relied on. That the present danger is imminent, no man can conceal. If war must come—if the bayonet must be used to maintain the Constitution—I can say before God my conscience is clean. I have struggled long for a peaceful solution of the difficulty. I have not only tendered those States what was theirs of right, but I have gone to the very extreme of magnanimity.

The return we receive is war, armies marched upon our capital, obstructions and dangers to our navigation, letters of marque to invite pirates to prey upon our commerce, a concerted movement to blot out the United States of America from the map of the globe. The question is, Are we to maintain the country of our fathers, or allow it to be stricken down by those who, when they can no longer govern, threaten to destroy?

What cause, what excuse do disunionists give us for breaking up the best Government on which the sun of heaven ever shed its rays? They are dissatisfied with the result of a Presidential election. Did they never get beaten before? Are we to resort to the sword when we get defeated at the ballot box? I understand it that the voice of the people expressed in the mode appointed by the Constitution must command the obedience of every citizen. They assume, on the election of a particular candidate, that their rights are not safe in the Union. What evidence do they present of this? I defy any man to show any act on which it is based. What act has been omitted to be done? I appeal to these assembled thousands that so far as the constitutional rights of the Southern States, I will say the constitutional rights of slaveholders, are concerned, nothing has been done, and nothing omitted, of which they can complain.

There has never been a time from the day that Washington was inaugurated first President of these United States, when the rights of the Southern States stood firmer under the laws of the land than they do now; there never was a time when they had not as good a cause for disunion as they have to-day. What good cause have they now that has not existed under every Administration?

If they say the Territorial question—now, for the first time, there is no act of Congress prohibiting slavery anywhere. If it be the non-enforcement of the laws, the only complaints that I have heard have been of the too vigorous and faithful fulfilment of the Fugitive Slave Law. Then what reason have they?

The slavery question is a mere excuse. The election of Lincoln is a mere pretext. The present secession movement is the result of an enormous conspiracy formed more than a year since—formed by leaders in the Southern Confederacy more than twelve months ago.

They use the Slavery question as a means to aid the accomplishment of their ends. They desired the election of a Northern candidate, by a sectional vote, in order to show that the two sections cannot live together. When the history of the two years from the Lecompton charter down to the Presidential election shall be written, it will be shown that the scheme was deliberately made to break up this Union.

They desired a Northern Republican to be elected by a purely Northern vote, and then assign this fact as a reason why the sections may not longer live together. If the disunion candidate in the late Presidential contest had carried the united South, their scheme was, the Northern candidate successful, to seize the Capital last spring, and by a united South and divided North hold it. That scheme was defeated in the defeat of the disunion candidate in several of the Southern States.

But this is no time for a detail of causes. The conspiracy is now known. Armies have been raised, war is levied to accomplish it. There are only two sides to the question. Every man must be for the United States or against it. There can be no neutrals in this war; *only patriots—or traitors.*

Thank God, Illinois is not divided on this question. (Cheers.) I know they expected to present a united South against a divided North. They hoped in the Northern States, party questions would bring civil war between Democrats and Republicans, when the South would step in with her cohorts, aid one party to conquer the other, and then make easy prey of the victors. Their scheme was carnage and civil war in the North.

There is but one way to defeat this. In Illinois it is being so defeated by closing up the ranks. War will thus be prevented on our own soil. While there was a hope of peace, I was ready for any reasonable sacrifice or compromise to maintain it. But when the question comes of war in the cotton-fields of the South, or the corn-fields of Illinois, I say the farther off the better.

We can not close our eyes to the sad and solemn fact that war does exist. The Government must be maintained, its enemies overthrown, and the more stupendous our preparations the less the bloodshed, and the shorter the struggle. But we must remember certain restraints on our action even in time of war. We are a Christian people, and the war must be prosecuted in a manner recognized by Christian nations.

We must not invade Constitutional rights. The innocent must not suffer, nor women and children be the victims. Savages must not be let loose. But while I sanction no war on the rights of others, I will implore my countrymen not to lay down their arms until our own rights are recognized. (Cheers.)

The Constitution and its guarantees are our birthright, and I am ready to enforce that inalienable right to the last extent. We can not recognize secession. Recognize it once, and you have not only dissolved government, but you have destroyed social order—upturned the foundations of society. You have inaugurated anarchy in its worst form, and will shortly experience all the horrors of the French Revolution.

Then we have a solemn duty—to maintain the Government. The greater our unanimity, the speedier the day of peace. We have prejudices to overcome from the few short months since of a fierce party contest. Yet these must be allayed. Let us lay aside all criminations and recriminations as to the origin of these difficulties. When we shall have again a country with the United States flag floating over it, and respected on every inch of American soil, it will then be time enough to ask who and what brought all this upon us.

I have said more than I intended to say. (Cries of "Go on.") It is a sad task to discuss questions so fearful as civil war; but sad as it is, bloody and disastrous as I expect it will be, I express it as my conviction before God, that it is the duty of every American citizen to rally round the flag of his country.

I thank you again for this magnificent demonstration. By it you show you have laid aside party strife. Illinois has a proud position—United, firm, determined never to permit the Government to be destroyed. (Prolonged cheering.)

PRESIDENT LINCOLN'S FIRST CALL FOR TROOPS.

APRIL 15TH, 1861.

Whereas, the laws of the United States have been for some time past, and now are, opposed, and the execution thereof obstructed, in the States of South Carolina, Georgia, Alabama, Florida, Mississippi, Louisiana, and Texas, by combinations too powerful to be suppressed by the ordinary course of judicial proceedings, or by the powers vested in the marshals by law ; now, therefore, I, Abraham Lincoln, President of the United States, in virtue of the power in me vested by the Constitution and the laws, have thought fit to call forth the Militia of the several States of the Union to the aggregate number of 75,000, in order to suppress said combinations, and to cause the laws to be duly executed.

The details for this object will be immediately communicated to the State authorities through the

War Department. I appeal to all loyal citizens to favor, facilitate, and aid, this effort to maintain the honor, the integrity, and existence, of our national Union, and the perpetuity of popular government, and to redress wrongs already long enough endured. I deem it proper to say that the first service assigned to the forces hereby called forth will probably be to repossess the forts, places, and property which have been seized from the Union; and in every event the utmost care will be observed, consistently with the objects aforesaid, to avoid any devastation, any destruction of, or interference with property, or any disturbance of peaceful citizens of any part of the country; and I hereby command the persons composing the combinations aforesaid, to disperse and retire peaceably to their respective abodes, within twenty days from this date.

Deeming that the present condition of public affairs presents an extraordinary occasion, I do hereby, in virtue of the power in me vested by the Constitution, convene both houses of Congress. The Senators and Representatives are, therefore, summoned to assemble at their respective chambers at twelve o'clock, noon, on Thursday, the fourth day of July next, then and there to consider and determine such measures as, in their wisdom, the public safety and interest may seem to demand.

In witness whereof, I have hereunto set my hand, and caused the seal of the United States to be affixed.

Done at the City of Washington, this fifteenth day of April, in the year of our Lord, one thousand eight hundred and sixty-one, and of the independence of the United States the eighty-fifth.

ABRAHAM LINCOLN.

By the President.

WILLIAM H. SEWARD, *Secretary of State.*

TOTAL NUMBER OF TROOPS CALLED INTO SERVICE DURING THE REBELLION.

THE various calls of the President for men were as follows:

1861,—3 months' men, ...	75,000
1861,—3 years' men, ...	500,000
1862,—3 years' men, ...	300,000
1862,—9 months' men, ...	300,000
1864,—3 years' men, February, . . .	500,000
1864,—3 years' men, March, . . .	200,000
1864,—3 years' men, July, . . .	500,000
1864,—3 years' men, December, . .	300,000
Total, ...	2,675,000

These do not include the militia that were brought into service during the various invasions of Lee's armies into Maryland and Pennsylvania.

RESOLUTIONS OF THE N. Y. CHAMBER OF COMMERCE.

SUSTAINING THE FEDERAL GOVERNMENT AND URGING A STRICT BLOCKADE OF SOUTHERN PORTS, APRIL 19TH, 1861.

Whereas, Our country has, in the course of events, reached a crisis unprecedented in its past history, exposing it to extreme dangers, and involving the most momentous results; and *Whereas*, The President of the United States has, by his Proclamation, made known the dangers which threaten the stability of Government, and called upon the people to rally in support of the Constitution and laws; and *Whereas*, The merchants of New York, represented in this Chamber, have a deep stake in the results which may flow from the present exposed state of national affairs, as well as a jealous regard for the honor of that flag under whose protection they have extended the commerce of this city to the remotest part of the world; therefore,

Resolved, That this Chamber, alive to the perils which have been gathering around our cherished form of Government and menacing its overthrow, has witnessed with lively satisfaction the determination of the President to maintain the Constitution and vindicate the supremacy of Government and law at every hazard. (Cheers.)

Resolved, That the so-called secession of some of the Southern States having at last culminated in open war against the United States, the American people can no longer defer their decision between anarchy or despotism on the one side, and on the other liberty, order, and law under the most benign Government the world has ever known.

Resolved, That this Chamber, forgetful of past differences of political opinion among its members, will, with unanimity and patriotic ardor, support the Government in this great crisis: and it hereby pledges its best efforts to sustain its credit and facilitate its financial operations. It also confidently appeals to all men of wealth to join in these efforts. (Applause.)

Resolved, That while deploring the advent of civil war which has been precipitated on the country by the madness of the South, the Chamber is persuaded that policy and humanity alike demand that it should be met by the most prompt and energetic measures; and it accordingly recommends to Government the instant adoption and prosecution of a policy so vigorous and resistless, that it will crush out treason now and forever. (Applause.)

Resolved, That the proposition of Mr. Jefferson Davis to issue letters of marque to whosoever may apply for them, emanating from no recognized Government, is not only without the sanction of public law, but piratical in its tendencies, and therefore deserving the stern condemnation of the civilized world. It cannot result in the fitting out of regular privateers, but may, in infesting the ocean with piratical cruisers, armed with traitorous commissions, to despoil our commerce and that of all other maritime nations. (Applause.)

Resolved, That in view of this threatening evil, it is, in the opinion of this Chamber, the duty of our Government to issue at once a proclamation, warning all persons, that privateering under the commissions proposed will be dealt with as simple piracy. It owes this duty not merely to itself, but to other maritime nations, who have a right to demand that the United States Government shall promptly discountenance every attempt within its borders to legalize piracy. It should, also, at the earliest moment, blockade every Southern port, so as to prevent the egress and ingress of such vessels. (Immense applause.)

Resolved, That the Secretary be directed to send copies of these resolutions to the Chambers of Commerce of other cities, inviting their co-operation in such measures as may be deemed effective in strengthening the hands of Government in this emergency.

Resolved, That a copy of these resolutions, duly attested by the officers of the Chamber, be forwarded to the President of the United States.

BLOCKADE RESOLUTIONS.

Whereas, War against the Constitution and Government of these United States has been commenced, and is carried on by certain combinations of individuals, assuming to act for States at the South claiming to have seceded from the United States; and

Whereas, Such combinations have officially promulgated an invitation for the enrollment of vessels, to act under their authorization, and as so-called "privateers," against the flag and commerce of the United States; therefore,

Resolved, by the Chamber of Commerce of the State of New York, That the United States Government be recommended and urged to blockade the ports of such States, or any other State that shall join them, and that this measure is demanded for defence in war, as also for protection to the commerce of the United States against these so-called "privateers" invited to enrol under the authority of such States.

Resolved, That the Chamber of Commerce of the State of New York pledges its hearty and cordial support to such measures as the Government of the United States may, in its wisdom, inaugurate and carry through in the blockade of such ports.

A PROCLAMATION,

BY THE PRESIDENT OF THE UNITED STATES OF AMERICA, BLOCKADING THE SOUTHERN PORTS.

Whereas an insurrection against the Government of the United States has broken out in the States of South Carolina, Georgia, Alabama, Florida, Mississippi, Louisiana, and Texas, and the laws of the United States for the collection of the revenue can not be efficiently executed therein conformably to that provision of the Constitution which requires duties to be uniform throughout the United States:

And *Whereas* a combination of persons, engaged in such insurrection, have threatened to grant pretended letters of marque to authorize the bearers thereof to commit assaults on the lives, vessels, and property of good citizens of the country lawfully engaged in commerce on the high seas, and in waters of the United States:

And *Whereas* an Executive Proclamation has

been already issued, requiring the persons engaged in these disorderly proceedings to desist therefrom, calling out a militia force for the purpose of repressing the same, and convening Congress in extraordinary session to deliberate and determine thereon:

Now, therefore, I, Abraham Lincoln, President of the United States, with a view to the same purposes before mentioned, and to the protection of the public peace, and the lives and property of quiet and orderly citizens pursuing their lawful occupations, until Congress shall have assembled and deliberated on the said unlawful proceedings, or until the same shall have ceased, have further deemed advisable to set on foot a Blockade of the ports within the States aforesaid, in pursuance of the laws of the United States and of the laws of nations in such cases provided. For this purpose a competent force will be posted so as to prevent entrance and exit of vessels from the ports aforesaid. If, therefore, with a view to violate such Blockade, a vessel shall approach, or shall attempt to leave any of the said ports, she will be duly warned by the Commander of one of the blockading vessels, who will endorse on her register the fact and date of such warning; and if the same vessel shall again attempt to enter or leave the blockaded port, she will be captured and sent to the nearest convenient port, for such proceedings against her and her cargo as prize as may be deemed advisable.

And I hereby proclaim and declare, that if any person, under the pretended authority of said States, or under any other pretence, shall molest a vessel of the United States, or the persons or cargo on board of her, such person will be held amenable to the laws of the United States for the prevention and punishment of piracy.

Abraham Lincoln.

By the President.

William H. Seward, *Secretary of State.*

Washington, April 19, 1861.

THE EMANCIPATION PROCLAMATION.

BY THE PRESIDENT OF THE UNITED STATES OF AMERICA.

WHEREAS, on the twenty-second day of September, in the year of our Lord one thousand eight hundred and sixty-two, a Proclamation was issued by the President of the United States, containing among other things the following, to wit:

"That on the first day of January, in the year of our Lord one thousand eight hundred and sixty-three, all persons held as slaves within any State, or designated part of a State, the people whereof shall then be in rebellion against the United States, shall be then, thenceforth and FOREVER FREE, and the Executive Government of the United States, including the military and naval authorities thereof, will recognize and maintain the freedom of such persons, and will do no act or acts to repress such persons, or any of them, in any efforts they may make for their actual freedom.

"That the Executive will, on the first day of

January aforesaid, by proclamation, designate the States and parts of States, if any, in which the people thereof respectively shall then be in rebellion against the United States, and the fact that any State, or the people thereof, shall on that day be in good faith represented in the Congress of the United States by members chosen thereto at elections wherein a majority of the qualified voters of such State shall have participated, shall, in the absence of strong countervailing testimony, be deemed conclusive evidence that such State and the people thereof are not then in rebellion against the United States."

Now, therefore, I, ABRAHAM LINCOLN, President of the United States, by virtue of the power in me vested as Commander-in-Chief of the Army and Navy of the United States in time of actual armed rebellion against the authority and government of the United States, and as a fit and necessary war measure for suppressing said rebellion, do, on this first day of January, in the year of our Lord one thousand eight hundred and sixty-three, and in accordance with my purpose so to do, publicly proclaim for the full period of one hundred days from the day of the first above mentioned order, and designate, as the States and parts of States wherein the people thereof respectively are this day in rebellion against the United States, the following, to wit:

ARKANSAS, TEXAS, LOUISIANA, (except the Parishes of St. Bernard, Plaquemines, Jefferson, St. John, St. Charles, St. James, Ascension, Assumption, Terre Bonne, Lafourche, St. Mary, St. Martin, and Orleans, including the City of Orleans), MISSISSIPPI, ALABAMA, FLORIDA, GEORGIA, SOUTH CAROLINA, NORTH CAROLINA, and VIRGINIA (except the forty-eight counties designated as West Virginia, and also the counties of Berkley, Accomac, Northampton, Elizabeth City, York, Princess Ann, and Norfolk, including the cities of Norfolk and Portsmouth), and which excepted parts are, for the present, left precisely as if this Proclamation were not issued.

And by virtue of the power and for the purpose aforesaid, I do order and declare that ALL PERSONS HELD AS SLAVES within said designated States and parts of States ARE, AND HENCEFORWARD SHALL BE FREE! and that the Executive Government of the United States, including the military and naval authorities thereof, will recognize and maintain the freedom of said persons.

And I hereby enjoin upon the people so declared to be free, to abstain from all violence, unless in necessary self-defence, and I recommend to them that in all cases, when allowed, they labor faithfully for reasonable wages.

And I further declare and make known that such persons of suitable condition will be received into the armed service of the United States to garrison forts, positions, stations and other places, and to man vessels of all sorts in said service.

And upon this act, sincerely believed to be an act of justice, warranted by the Constitution, upon military necessity, I invoke the considerate judgment of mankind and the gracious favor of Almighty God.

In testimony whereof I have hereunto set my name, and caused the seal of the United States to be affixed.

Done at the City of Washington, this first day of January, in the year of our Lord one [L. S.] thousand eight hundred and sixty-three, and of the Independence of the United States the eighty-seventh.

ABRAHAM LINCOLN.

By the President.

WILLIAM H. SEWARD,

Secretary of State.

THE CONFISCATION ACT.

TO CONFISCATE PROPERTY USED FOR INSURRECTIONARY PURPOSES.

Be it enacted, etc., That if, during the present or any future insurrection against the Government of the United States, after the President of the United States shall have declared, by proclamation, that the laws of the United States are opposed, and the execution thereof obstructed, by combinations too powerful to be suppressed by the ordinary course of judicial proceedings, or by the power vested in the marshals by law, any person or persons, his, her, or their agent, attorney, or employee, shall purchase or acquire, sell or give any property of whatsoever kind or description, with intent to use or employ the same, or suffer the same to be used or employed, in aiding, abetting, or promoting such insurrection or resistance to the laws, or any person or persons engaged therein; or if any person or persons, being the owner or owners of any such property, shall knowingly use or employ, or consent to the use or employment of the same as aforesaid, all such property is hereby declared to be lawful subject of prize and capture wherever found; and it shall be the duty of the President of the United States to cause the same to be seized, confiscated, and condemned.

SEC. 2. Such prizes and capture shall be condemned in the district or circuit court of the United States, having jurisdiction of the amount, or in admiralty in any district in which the same may be seized, or into which they may be taken and proceedings first instituted.

SEC. 3. The Attorney-General, or any district attorney of the United States in which said property may at the time be, may institute the proceedings of condemnation, and in such case they shall be wholly for the benefit of the United States; or any person may file an information with such attorney, in which case the proceedings shall be for the use of such informer and the United States in equal parts.

SEC. 4. Whenever hereafter, during the present insurrection against the Government of the United States, any person claimed to be held to labor or service under the law of any State, shall be required or permitted by the person to whom such labor or service is claimed to be due, or by the lawful agent of such persons, to take up arms against the United States, or shall be required or permitted by the person to whom such labor or service is claimed to be due, or his lawful agent, to work or to be employed in or upon any fort, navy yard, dock, armory, ship, intrenchment, or in any military or naval service whatsoever, against the Government and lawful authority of the United States, then, and in every such case, the person to whom such labor or service is claimed to be due, shall forfeit his claim to such labor, any law of the State or of the United States to the contrary notwithstanding. And whenever thereafter the person claiming such labor or service shall seek to enforce his claim, it shall be a full and sufficient answer to such claim that the person whose service or labor is claimed had been employed in the hostile service against the Government of the United States, contrary to the provisions of this act.

FIRST INAUGURAL ADDRESS OF PRESIDENT LINCOLN

MARCH 4TH, 1861.

Fellow-Citizens of the United States:

In compliance with a custom as old as the Government itself, I appear before you to address you briefly, and to take, in your presence, the oath prescribed by the Constitution of the United States to be taken by the President, before he enters on the execution of his office.

I do not consider it necessary, at present, for me to discuss those matters of administration about which there is no special anxiety or excitement. Apprehension seems to exist among the people of the Southern States, that, by the accession of a Republican Administration, their property and their peace and personal security are to be endangered. There has never been any reasonable cause for such apprehension. Indeed, the most ample evidence to the contrary has all the while existed, and been open to their inspection. It is found in nearly all the published speeches of him who now addresses you. I do but quote from one of those speeches, when I declare that "I have no purpose, directly or indirectly, to interfere with the institution of slavery in the States where it exists." I believe I have no lawful right to do so; and I have no inclination to do so. Those who nominated and elected me, did so with the full knowledge that I had made this, and made many similar declarations, and had never recanted them. And, more than this, they placed in the platform, for my acceptance, and as a law to themselves and to me, the clear and emphatic resolution which I now read:

"*Resolved*, That the maintenance inviolate of the rights of the States, and especially the right of each State to order and control its own domestic institutions according to its own judgment exclusively, is essential to that balance of power on which the perfection and endurance of our political fabric depend; and we denounce the lawless invasion by armed force of the soil of any State or Territory, no matter under what pretext, as among the gravest of crimes."

I now reiterate these sentiments; and in doing so I only press upon the public attention the most conclusive evidence of which the case is susceptible, that the property, peace, and security of no section are to be in anywise endangered by the now incoming Administration.

I add, too, that all the protection which, consistently with the Constitution and the laws, can be given will be cheerfully given to all the States when lawfully demanded, for whatever cause, as cheerfully to one section as to another.

There is much controvery about the delivering up of fugitives from service or labor. The clause I now read is as plainly written in the Constitution as any other of its provisions:

"No person held to service or labor in one State under the laws thereof, escaping into another, shall, in consequence of any law or regulation therein, be discharged from such service or labor, but shall be delivered up on claim of the party to whom such service or labor may be due."

It is scarcely questioned that this provision was intended by those who made it for the reclaiming of what we call fugitive slaves; and the intention of the lawgiver is the law.

All members of Congress swear their support to the whole Constitution—to this provision as well as any other. To the proposition, then, that slaves whose cases come within the terms of this clause "shall be delivered up," their oaths are unanimous. Now, if they would make the effort in good temper, could they not, with nearly equal unanimity, frame and pass a law by means of which to keep good that unanimous oath?

There is some difference of opinion whether this clause should be enforced by National or by State authority; but surely that difference is not a very material one. If the slave is to be surrendered, it can be of but little consequence to him or to others by which authority it is done; and should any one, in any case, be content that this oath shall go unkept on a merely unsubstantial controversy as to how it shall be kept?

Again, in any law upon this subject, ought not all the safeguards of liberty known in the civilized and humane jurisprudence to be introduced, so that a free man be not, in any case, surrendered as a slave? And might it not be well at the same time to provide by law for the enforcement of that clause in the Constitution which guaranties that "the citizens of each State shall be entitled to all the privileges and immunities of citizens of the several States?"

I take the official oath to-day with no mental

reservations, and with no purpose to construe the Constitution or laws by any hypercritical rules; and while I do not choose now to specify particular acts of Congress as proper to be enforced, I do suggest that it will be much safer for all, both in official and private stations, to conform to and abide by all those acts which stand unrepealed, than to violate any of them, trusting to find impunity in having them held to be unconstitutional.

It is seventy-two years since the first inauguration of a President under our national Constitution. During that period fifteen different and very distinguished citizens have in succession administered the executive branch of the government. They have conducted it through many perils, and generally with great success. Yet, with all this scope for precedent, I now enter upon the same task, for the brief constitutional term of four years, under great and peculiar difficulties.

A disruption of the Federal Union, heretofore only menaced, is now formidably attempted. I hold that in the contemplation of universal law and of the Constitution, the Union of these States is perpetual. Perpetuity is implied, if not expressed, in the fundamental law of all national governments. It is safe to assert that no government proper ever had a provision in its organic law for its own termination. Continue to execute all the express provisions of our national Constitution, and the Union will endure forever, it being impossible to destroy it, except by some action not provided for in the instrument itself.

Again, if the United States be not a government proper, but an association of States in the nature of a contract merely, can it, as a contract, be peaceably unmade by less than all the parties who made it? One party to a contract may violate it—break it, so to speak; but does it not require all to lawfully rescind it? Descending from these general principles we find the proposition that in legal contemplation the Union is perpetual, confirmed by the history of the Union itself.

The Union is much older than the Constitution. It was formed, in fact, by the Articles of Association in 1774. It was matured and continued in the Declaration of Independence in 1776. It was further matured, and the faith of all the then thirteen States expressly plighted and engaged that it should be perpetual, by the Articles of Confederation, in 1778; and, finally, in 1787, one of the declared objects for ordaining and establishing the Constitution was to form a more perfect Union. But if the destruction of the Union by one or by a part only of the States be lawfully possible, the Union is less than before, the Constitution having lost the vital element of perpetuity.

It follows from these views that no State, upon its own mere motion, can lawfully get out of the Union; that resolves and ordinances to that effect, are legally void; and that acts of violence within any State or States against the authority of the United States, are insurrectionary or revolutionary, according to circumstances.

I therefore consider that, in view of the Constitution and the laws, the Union is unbroken, and, to the extent of my ability, I shall take care, as the Constitution itself expressly enjoins upon me, that the laws of the Union shall be faithfully executed in all the States. Doing this, which I deem to be only a simple duty on my part, I shall perfectly perform it, so far as is practicable, unless my rightful masters, the American people, shall withhold the requisition, or in some authoritative manner direct the contrary.

I trust this will not be regarded as a menace, but only as the declared purpose of the Union that it will constitutionally defend and maintain itself.

In doing this there need be no bloodshed or violence, and there shall be none unless it is forced upon the national authority.

The power confided to me *will be used to hold, occupy, and possess the property and places belonging to the Government*, and collect the duties and imposts; but beyond what may be necessary for these objects there will be no invasion, no using of force against or among the people anywhere.

Where hostility to the United States shall be so great and so universal as to prevent competent resident citizens from holding the Federal offices, there will be no attempt to force obnoxious strangers among the people that object. While the strict legal right may exist of the Government to enforce the exercise of these offices, the attempt to do so would be so irritating, and so nearly impracticable withal, that I deem it better to forego for the time the uses of such offices.

The mails, unless repelled, will continue to be furnished in all parts of the Union.

So far as possible, the people everywhere shall have that sense of perfect security which is most favorable to calm thought and reflection.

The course here indicated will be followed, unless current events and experience shall show a modification or change to be proper; and in every case and exigency my best discretion will be exercised according to the circumstances actually existing, and with a view and hope of a peaceful solution of the national troubles, and the restoration of fraternal sympathies and affections.

That there are persons, in one section or another, who seek to destroy the Union at all events, and are glad of any pretext to do it, I will neither affirm nor deny. But if there be such, I need address no word to them.

To those, however, who really love the Union, may I not speak, before entering upon so grave a matter as the destruction of our national fabric, with all its benefits, its memories, and its hopes? Would it not be well to ascertain why we do it? Will you hazard so desperate a step, while any portion of the ills you fly from, have no real existence? Will you, while the certain ills you fly to, are greater than all the real ones you fly from? Will you risk the commission of so fearful a mistake? All profess to be content in the Union if all constitutional rights can be maintained. Is it true, then, that any right, plainly written in the Constitution has been denied? I think not. Happily the human mind is so constituted, that no party can reach to the audacity of doing this.

Think, if you can, of a single instance in which a plainly-written provision of the Constitution has ever been denied. If, by the mere force of numbers, a majority should deprive a minority of any clearly-written constitutional right, it might, in a moral point of view, justify revolution; it certainly would, if such right were a vital one. But such is not our case.

All the vital rights of minorities and of individuals are so plainly assured to them by affirmations and negations, guaranties and prohibitions in the Constitution, that controversies never arise concerning them. But no organic law can ever be framed with a provision specifically applicable to every question which may occur in practical administration. No foresight can anticipate, nor any document of reasonable length contain, express provisions for all possible questions. Shall fugitives from labor be surrendered by national or by State authorities? The Constitution does not expressly say. Must Congress protect slavery in the Territories? The Constitution does not expressly say. From questions of this class, spring all our constitutional controversies, and we divide upon them into majorities and minorities.

If the minority will not acquiesce, the majority must, or the government must cease. There is no alternative for continuing the government but acquiescence on the one side or the other. If a minority in such a case, will secede rather than acquiesce, they make a precedent which in turn will ruin and divide them, for a minority of their own will secede from them whenever a majority refuses to be controlled by such a minority. For instance, why not any portion of a new confederacy, a year or two hence, arbitrarily secede again, precisely as portions of the present Union now claim to secede from it? All who cherish disunion sentiments are now being educated to the exact temper of doing this. Is there such perfect identity of interests among the States to compose a new Union as to produce harmony only, and prevent renewed secession? Plainly, the central idea of secession is the essence of anarchy.

A majority held in restraint by constitutional check and limitation, and always changing easily with deliberate changes of popular opinions and sentiments, is the only true sovereign of a free people. Whoever rejects it, does, of necessity, fly to anarchy or to despotism. Unanimity is impossible; and the rule of a majority, as a permanent arrangement, is wholly inadmissible. So that, rejecting the majority principle, anarchy or despotism in some form is all that is left.

I do not forget the position assumed by some that constitutional questions are to be decided by the Supreme Court, nor do I deny that such decisions must be binding in any case upon the parties to a suit, as to the object of that suit, while they are also entitled to very high respect and consideration in all parallel cases by all other departments of the government; and while it is obviously possible that such decision may be erroneous in any given case, still the evil effect following it, being limited to that particular case, with the chance that it may be overruled and never become a precedent for other cases, can better be borne than could the evils of a different practice.

At the same time the candid citizen must confess that if the policy of the government upon the vital questions affecting the whole people is to be irrevocably fixed by the decisions of the Supreme Court, the instant they are made, as in ordinary litigation between parties in personal actions, the people will have ceased to be their own masters, unless having to that extent practically resigned their government into the hands of that eminent tribunal.

Nor is there in this view any assault upon the court or the judges. It is a duty from which they may not shrink, to decide cases properly brought before them; and it is no fault of theirs if others seek to turn their decisions into political purposes. One section of our country believes slavery is right and ought to be extended, while the other believes it is wrong and ought not to be extended; and this is the only substantial dispute; and the fugitive slave clause of the Constitution, and the law for the suppression of the foreign slave trade, are each as well enforced, perhaps, as any law can ever be in a community where the moral sense of the people imperfectly supports the law itself. The great body of the people abide by the dry legal obligation in both cases, and a few break over in each. This, I think, cannot be perfectly cured, and it would be worse in both cases after the separation of the sections than before. The foreign slave trade, now imperfectly suppressed, would be ultimately revived, without restriction, in one section; while fugitive slaves, now only partially surrendered, would not be surrendered at all by the other.

Physically speaking we cannot separate— we cannot remove our respective sections from each other, nor build an impassable wall between them. A husband and wife may be divorced, and go out of the presence and beyond the reach of each other, but the different sections of our country cannot do this. They cannot but remain face to face; and intercourse, either amicable or hostile, must continue between them. Is it possible, then, to make that intercourse more advantageous or more satisfactory after separation than before? Can aliens make treaties easier than friends can make laws? Can treaties be more faithfully enforced between aliens than laws can among friends? Suppose you go to war, you cannot fight always; and when, after much loss on both sides and no gain on either, you cease fighting, the identical questions as to terms of intercourse are again upon you.

This country, with its institutions, belongs to the people who inhabit it. Whenever they shall grow weary of the existing government, they can exercise their constitutional right of amending, or their revolutionary right to dismember or overthrow it. I cannot be ignorant of the fact that many worthy and patriotic citizens are desirous of having the national Constitution amended. While I make no recommendation of amendment, I fully recognize the full authority of the people over the whole subject, to be exercised in either of the modes prescribed in the instrument itself, and I should, under existing circumstances, favor, rather than oppose, a fair opportunity being afforded the people to act upon it.

I will venture to add, that to me the convention mode seems preferable, in that it allows amendments to originate with the people themselves, instead of only permitting them to take or reject propositions originated by others not especially chosen for the purpose, and which might not be precisely such as they would wish either to accept or refuse. I understand that a proposed amendment to the Constitution (which amendment, however, I have not seen) has passed Congress, to the effect that the Federal Government shall never interfere with the domestic institutions of States, including that of persons held to service. To avoid misconstruction of what I have said, I depart from my purpose not to speak of particular amendments, so far as to say that, holding such a provision to now be implied constitutional law, I have no objection to its being made express and irrevocable.

The chief magistrate derives all his authority from the people, and they have conferred none upon him to fix the terms for the separation of the States. The people themselves, also, can do this if they choose, but the Executive, as such, has nothing to do with it. His duty is to administer the present government as it came to his hands, and to transmit it unimpaired by him to his successor. Why should there not be a patient confidence in the ultimate justice of the people? Is there any better or equal hope in the world? In our present differences is either party without faith of being in the right? If the Almighty Ruler of nations, with his eternal truth and justice, be on your side of the North, or on yours of the South, that truth and that justice will surely prevail by the judgment of this great tribunal, the American people. By the frame of the Government under which we live, this same people have wisely given their public servants but little power for mischief, and have with equal wisdom provided for the return of that little to their own hands at very short intervals. While the people retain their virtue and vigilance, no administration, by any extreme wickedness or folly, can very seriously injure the Government in the short space of four years.

My countrymen, one and all, think calmly and well upon this whole subject. Nothing valuable can be lost by taking time.

If there be an object to hurry any of you, in hot haste, to a step which you would never take deliberately, that object will be frustrated by taking time; but no good object can be frustrated by it.

Such of you as are now dissatisfied still have the old Constitution unimpaired, and on the sensitive point, the laws of your own framing under it; while the new administration will have no immediate power, if it would, to change either.

If it were admitted that you who are dissatisfied hold the right side in the dispute, there is still no single reason for precipitate action. Intelligence, patriotism, Christianity, and a firm reliance on Him who has never yet forsaken this favored land, are still competent to adjust, in the best way, all our present difficulties.

In your hands, my dissatisfied fellow-countrymen, and not in mine, is the momentous issue of civil war. The government will not assail you.

You can have no conflict without being yourselves the aggressors. You have no oath registered in Heaven to destroy the government; while I shall have the most solemn one to "preserve, protect, and defend it."

I am loath to close. We are not enemies, but friends. We must not be enemies. Though passion may have strained, it must not break our bonds of affection.

The mystic cords of memory, stretching from every battle-field and patriot grave to every living heart and hearthstone all over this broad land, will yet swell the chorus of the Union, when again touched, as surely they will be, by the better angels of our nature.

THE BALANCE SHEET OF THE GOVERNMENT,

BEFORE AND SINCE THE WAR, 1859 AND 1865.

The receipts into the Treasury during the fiscal year ending June 30, 1859, were as follows:

From Customs	$49,565,824 38
From Public Lands	1,756,687 30
From Miscellaneous Sources	2,082,559 33
From Treasury Notes	9,667,400 00
From Loans	18,620,000 00
Aggregate resources for the year ending June 30, 1859	$88,090,787 11

Which amount was expended as follows:

Civil, Foreign and Miscellan's.	$23,635,820 94	
Interior (Indians and Pensions),	4,753,972 60	
War Department	23,243,822 38	
Navy Department	14,712,610 21	
Public Debt	17,405,285 44	
Total expenses for the year		$83,751,511 57
Balance in Treasury July 1, 1859		4,339,275 54

The receipts into the Treasury during the fiscal year ending June 30, 1865, was $1,898,532,533 24, of which were received:

From loans applied to expenses	$864,863.499 17
From loans applied to Public Debt	607,361,241 68
From Internal Revenue	209,464,215 25
Expenditures for the year	$1,897,674,224 09
War Department charged with	1,031,323,360 79
Balance in Treasury July 1, 1865	858,309 15
Total increase of Public Debt during the year	941,902,537 04

PRESIDENT LINCOLN'S SECOND AND LAST INAUGURAL ADDRESS.

MARCH 4, 1865.

FELLOW-COUNTRYMEN: At this second appearing to take the oath of the Presidential office, there is less occasion for an extended address than there was at the first. Then a statement, somewhat in detail, of a course to be pursued seemed very fitting and proper. Now, at the expiration of four years, during which public declarations have been constantly called forth on every point and phase of the great contest which still absorbs the attention and engrosses the energies of the nation, little that is new could be presented.

The progress of our arms, upon which all else chiefly depends, is as well known to the public as to myself, and it is, I trust reasonably satisfactory and encouraging to all. With high hope for the future, no prediction in regard to it is ventured.

On the occasion corresponding to this four years ago, all thoughts were anxiously directed to an impending civil war. All dreaded it; all sought to avoid it. While the inaugural address was being delivered from this place, devoted altogether to saving the Union without war, insurgent agents were in the city seeking to destroy it without war—seeking to dissolve the Union and divide the effects by negotiation. Both parties deprecated war, but one of them would make war rather than let the nation survive; and the other would rather accept war than let it perish, and the war came.

One-eighth of the whole population were colored slaves, not distributed generally over the Union, but localized in the Southern part of it. These slaves constituted a peculiar and powerful interest. All knew that this interest was somehow the cause of the war. To strengthen, perpetuate, and extend this interest, was the object for which the insurgents would rend the Union even by war, while the Government claimed no right to do more than to restrict the territorial enlargement of it.

Neither party expected for the war the magnitude or the duration which it has already attained. Neither anticipated that the cause of the conflict might cease with, or even before the conflict itself should cease. Each looked for an easier triumph, and a result less fundamental and astounding.

Both read the same Bible, and pray to the same God; and each invoke his aid against the other. It may seem strange that any men should dare to ask a just God's assistance in wringing their bread from the sweat of other men's faces; but let us judge not, that we be not judged. The prayers of both could not be answered. That of neither has been answered fully. The Almighty has his own purposes. "Woe unto the world because of offences, for it must must needs be that offences come; but woe to that man by whom the offence cometh." If we shall suppose that American slavery is one of these offences, which, in the providence of God, must needs come, but which, having continued through his appointed time, he now wills to remove, and that he gives to both North and South this terrible war as the woe due to those by whom the offence came, shall we discern therein any departure from those divine attributes which the believers in a living God always ascribe to him? Fondly do we hope, fervently do we pray, that this mighty scourge of war may soon pass away. Yet, if God wills that it continue until all the wealth piled by the bondman's two hundred and fifty years of unrequited toil shall be sunk, and until every drop of blood drawn with the lash, shall be paid with another drawn by the sword; as was said three thousand years ago, so still it must be said, "The judgments of the Lord are true and righteous altogether."

With malice toward none, with charity to all, with firmness in the right, as God gives us to see the right, let us strive on to finish the work we are in; to bind up the nation's wounds; to care for him who shall have borne the battle, and for his widow and his orphans; to do all which may achieve and cherish a just and a lasting peace among ourselves and with all nations.

PRESIDENT LINCOLN'S PROCLAMATION OF AMNESTY.

ACCOMPANYING THE PRESIDENT'S MESSAGE, DECEMBER 8, 1863.

WHEREAS, in and by the Constitution of the United States, it is provided that the President "shall have power to grant reprieves and pardons for offences against the United States, except in cases of impeachment;" and whereas a rebellion now exists whereby the loyal State governments of several States have for a long time been subverted, and many persons have committed and are now guilty of treason against the United States; and whereas, with reference to said rebellion and treason, laws have been enacted by Congress declaring forfeitures and confiscation of property and liberation of slaves, all upon terms and conditions therein stated; and also declaring that the President was thereby authorized at any time thereafter, by proclamation, to extend to persons who may have participated in the existing rebellion, in any State or part thereof, pardon and amnesty, with such exceptions and at such times and on such conditions as he may deem expedient for the public welfare; and whereas the congressional declaration for limited and conditional pardon accords with well established judicial exposition of the pardoning power; and whereas, with reference to said rebellion, the President of the United States has issued several proclamations with provisions in regard to the liberation of slaves; and whereas it is now desired by some persons heretofore engaged in said rebellion to resume their allegiance to the United States, and to reinaugurate loyal State governments within and for their respective States: Therefore,

"I, ABRAHAM LINCOLN, President of the United States, do proclaim, declare, and make known to all persons who have, directly or by implication, participated in the existing rebellion, except as hereinafter excepted, that a full pardon is hereby granted to them and each of them, with restoration of all rights of property, except as to slaves, and in property cases where rights of third parties shall have intervened, and upon the condition that every such person shall take and subscribe an oath, and thenceforward keep and maintain such oath inviolate; and which oath shall be registered for permanent preservation, and shall be of the tenor and effect following, to wit:

"I, —— ———, do solemnly swear, in presence of Almighty God, that I will henceforth faithfully support, protect, and defend the Constitution of the United States, and the union of the States thereunder; and that I will in like manner, abide by and faithfully support all acts of Congress passed during the existing rebellion with reference to slaves, so long and so far as not repealed, modified, or held void by Congress, or by decision of the Supreme Court; and that I will, in like manner, abide by and faithfully support all proclamations of the President made during the existing rebellion having reference to slaves, so long and so far as not modified or declared void by decision of the Supreme Court. So help me God."

The persons excepted from the benefits of the foregoing provisions are, all who are, or shall have been, civil or diplomatic officers or agents of the so-called confederate government; all who have left judicial stations under the United States to aid the rebellion; all who are, or shall have been, military or naval officers of said so-called confederate government, above the rank of colonel in the army, or of lieutenant in the navy; all who left seats in the United States Congress to aid the rebellion; all who resigned commissions in the Army or Navy of the United States, and afterwards aided the rebellion; and all who have engaged in any way in treating colored persons, or white persons in charge of such, otherwise than lawfully as prisoners of war, and which persons may have been found in the United States Service as soldiers, seamen, or in any other capacity.

And I do further proclaim, declare and make known, that whenever, in any of the States of Arkansas, Texas, Louisiana, Mississippi, Tennessee, Alabama, Georgia, Florida, South Carolina, and North Carolina, a number of persons. not less than one-tenth in number of the votes cast in such State at the presidential election of the year of our Lord 1860, each having taken the oath aforesaid, and not having since violated it, and being a qualified voter by the election law of the State existing immediately before the so-called act of secession, and excluding all others shall re-establish a State government which shall be republican, and in nowise contravening said oath, such shall be recognized as the true government of the State, and the State shall receive thereunder the benefits of the constitutional provision which declares that "the United States shall guaranty to every State in this Union a republican form of government, and shall protect each of them against invasion; and, on application of the Legislature, or the Executive (when the Legislature cannot be convened), against domestic violence."

And I do further proclaim, declare, and make known that any provision which may be adopted by such State government in relation to the freed people of such State, which shall recognize and declare their permanent freedom, provide for their education, and which may yet be consistent, as a temporary arrangement, with their present condition as a laboring, landless, and homeless class, will not be objected to by the National Executive. And it is suggested as not improper, that, in constructing a loyal State government in any State, the name of the State, the boundary, the subdivisions, the constitution, and the general code of laws, as before the rebellion, be maintained, subject only to the modifications made necessary by the conditions hereinbefore stated, and such others, if any, not contravening said conditions, and which may be deemed expedient by those framing the new State government.

To avoid misunderstanding, it may be proper to say that this proclamation, so far as it relates to State governments, has no reference to States wherein loyal State governments have all the while been maintained. And for the same reason, it may be proper to further say that whether members sent to Congress from any State shall be admitted to seats, constitutionally rests exclusive with the respective Houses, and not to any extent with the Executive. And still further, that this proclamation is intended to present the people of the States wherein the national authority has been suspended, and loyal State governments have been subverted, a mode in and by which the national authority and loyal State governments may be re-established within said States, or in any of them; and, while the mode presented is the best the Executive can suggest, with his present impressions, it must not be understood that no other possible mode would be acceptable.

Given under my hand, at the City of Washington, the 8th day of December, A. D. 1863, and of [L. S.] the independence of the United States of America the eighty-eighth.

ABRAHAM LINCOLN.

By the President.

WM. H. SEWARD, *Secretary of State.*

PRESIDENT JOHNSON'S AMNESTY PROCLAMATION.

BY THE PRESIDENT OF THE UNITED STATES OF AMERICA.

Whereas, The President of the United States, on the 8th day of December, 1863, did, with the object of suppressing the existing rebellion, to induce all persons to lay down their arms, to return to their loyalty, and to restore the authority of the United States, issue proclamations offering amnesty and pardon to certain persons who had directly or by implication, engaged in said rebellion; and

Whereas, Many persons who had so engaged in the late rebellion have, since the issuance of said proclamation, failed or neglected to take the benefits offered thereby; and

Whereas, Many persons who have been justly deprived of all claim to amnesty and pardon thereunder, by reason of their participation directly or by implication in said rebellion, and continued in hostility to the Government of the United States since the date of said proclamation, now desire to apply for and obtain amnesty and pardon:

To the end, therefore, that the authority of the Government of the United States may be restored, and that peace, and order, and freedom may be established, I, Andrew Johnson, President of the United States, do proclaim and declare, that I hereby grant to all persons who have directly or indirectly participated in the existing rebellion, except as hereafter excepted, amnesty and pardon, with restoration of all rights of property, except as to slaves, except in cases where legal proceedings under the laws of the United States, providing for the confiscation of property of persons engaged in rebellion, have been instituted, but on the condition, nevertheless, that every such person shall take and subscribe to the following oath, which shall be registered, for permanent preservation, and shall be of the tenor and effect following, to wit:

I do solemnly swear or affirm in presence of Almighty God, that I will henceforth support, protect, and faithfully defend the Constitution of the United States, and will, in like manner, abide by and faithfully support all laws and proclamations which have been made during the existing rebellion with reference to the emancipation of slaves. So help me God.

The following classes of persons are excepted from the benefits of this proclamation.

1. All who are or have been pretended diplomatic officers, or otherwise domestic or foreign agents of the pretended Confederate States.

2. All who left judicial stations under the United States to aid in the rebellion.

3. All who have been military or naval officers of the pretended Confederate Government above the rank of colonel in the army, and lieutenant in the navy.

4. All who left their seats in the Congress of the United States to aid in the rebellion.

5. All who resigned or tendered the resignation of their commissions in the army and navy of the United States to evade their duty in resisting the rebellion.

6. All who have engaged in any way in treating otherwise than lawfully as prisoners of war, persons found in the United States service as officers, soldiers, seamen, or in other capacities.

7. All persons who have been or are absentees from the United States for the purpose of aiding the rebellion.

8. All military or naval officers in the rebel service who were educated by the Government in the Military Academy at West Point, or at the United States Naval Academy.

9. All persons who held the pretended offices of Governors of the States in insurrection against the United States.

10. All persons who left their homes within the jurisdiction and protection of the United States, and passed beyond the Federal military lines into the so-called Confederate States for the purpose of aiding the rebellion.

11. All persons who have engaged in the destruction of the commerce of the United States upon the high seas, and all persons who have made raids into the United States from Canada, or been engaged in destroying the commerce of the United States on the lakes and rivers that separate the British provinces from the United States.

12. All persons who, at a time when they seek to obtain the benefits hereof by taking the oath herein prescribed, are in military, naval or civil confinement or custody, or under bond of the military or naval authorities or agents of the United States as prisoners of any kind, either before or after their conviction.

13. All persons who have voluntarily participated in said rebellion, the estimated value of whose taxable property is over twenty thousand dollars.

14. All persons who have taken the oath of amnesty, as prescribed in the President's proclamation

of December 8, 1863, or the oath of allegiance to the United States since the date of said proclamation, and who have not thenceforward kept the same inviolate; provided, that special application may be made to the President for pardon by any person belonging to the excepted classes, and such clemency will be extended as may be consistent with the facts of the case and the peace and dignity of the United States. The Secretary of State will establish rules and regulations for administering and recording the said amnesty oath, so as to insure its benefits to the people, and guard the government against fraud.

In testimony whereof, I have hereunto set my hand, and caused the seal of the United States to be affixed.

Done at the City of Washington, this the 29th day of May, 1865, and of the independence of America the 89th.

ANDREW JOHNSON.

By the President,

WM. H. SEWARD, *Secretary of State.*

A PEACE PROCLAMATION.

ON the 20th of August, 1866, the President issued a proclamation announcing the return of peace and restoring the writ of *habeas corpus* in all the Southern States. Among the points made in this proclamation are the following:

"There now exists no organized armed resistance of the misguided citizens or others to the authority of the United States in the States of Georgia, South Carolina, Virginia, North Carolina, Tennessee, Alabama, Louisiana, Arkansas, Mississippi, and Florida, and the laws can be sustained and enforced therein by the proper civil authority, State or Federal, and the people of the said States are well and loyally disposed, and have conformed, or will conform, in their legislation to the condition of affairs growing out of the amendment to the Constitution of the United

States prohibiting slavery within the jurisdiction of the United States.

"* * * The people of the several before mentioned States have, in the manner aforesaid, given satisfactory evidence that they acquiesce in this sovereign and important revolution of the national unity.

"It is believed to be a fundamental principle of government that people who have revolted, and who have been overcome and subdued, must either be dealt with so as to induce them voluntarily to become friends, or else they must be held by absolute military power, or devastated so as to prevent them from ever again doing harm as enemies, which last named policy is abhorrent to humanity and freedom.

"The Constitution of the United States provides for constitutional communities only as States, and not as territories, dependencies, provinces, or protectorates.

"* * * Therefore, I, Andrew Johnson, President of the United States, do hereby proclaim and declare that the insurrection which heretofore existed in the States of Georgia, South Carolina, North Carolina, Virginia, Tennessee, Alabama, Louisiana, Arkansas, Mississippi, and Florida is at an end, and henceforth to be so regarded."

CIVIL RIGHTS BILL.

AS ADOPTED BY CONGRESS, MARCH, 1866.

§ 1. That all persons in the United States, and not subject to any foreign power, excluding Indians not taxed, are hereby declared to be citizens of the United States; and such citizens of every race and color, without regard to any previous condition of Slavery or involuntary service, except as a punishment for crime, whereof the party shall have been duly convicted, shall have the same right, in every State and Territory, to make and enforce contracts, to sue, to be sued, be parties and give evidence; to inherit, purchase, lease, sell, hold, and convey personal property, and to full and equal benefit of all laws and proceedings for the security of person and property as are enjoyed by white citizens; and shall be subject to the like punishment, pains and penalties, and to none other; any law, statute, ordinance, regulation, or custom to the contrary notwithstanding.

§ 2. And that any person who, under color of any law, statute, ordinance, regulation, or custom, shall subject, or cause to be subjected, any inhabitant of any State or Territory to the deprivation of any right secured or protected by this act, or to punishment, pains, and penalties, on account of such person having at any time been held in a condition of slavery, or involuntary servitude, except for the punishment of crime whereof the party shall have been duly convicted, or by the reason of his color or race, than is prescribed for the punishment of white persons, shall be deemed guilty of a misdemeanor, and, on conviction, shall be punished by a fine not exceeding one thousand dollars, or imprisonment not exceeding one year, or both, in the discretion of the court.

§ 3. That the district courts of the United States, within their respective districts, shall have, exclusively of the courts of the several States, cognizance of all crimes and offences committed against the provisions of this act, and also, concurrently with the circuit courts of the United States, of all causes civil and criminal, affecting persons who are denied, or can not enforce in the courts of judicial tribunal of the State or locality where they may be, any of the rights secured to them by the first section of this act; and if any suit or prosecution, civil or criminal, has been, or shall be commenced in any State court against any such person, for any cause whatsoever, civil or military, or any other person, any arrest or imprisonment, trespasses, or wrong done or committed by virtue or under color of authority derived from this act, or the act establishing a bureau for the relief of freedmen and refugees, and all acts amendatory thereof, or for refusing to do any act, upon the ground that it would be inconsistent with this act, such defendant shall have the right to remove such cause for trial to the proper district or circuit court, in the manner prescribed by the act relating to *habeas corpus*, and regulating judicial proceedings in certain cases, approved March 3, 1863, and all acts amendatory thereto. The jurisdiction in civil and criminal matters hereby conferred on the district and circuit courts of the United States shall be exercised and enforced, in conformity with the laws of the United States, so far as such laws are suitable to carry the same into effect; but in all cases where such laws are not adapted to the object, or are deficient in the provisions necessary to furnish suitable remedies and punish offences against the law, the common law, as modified and changed by the Constitution and statutes of the State wherein the court having jurisdiction of the cause, civil or criminal, is held, so far as the same is not inconsistent with the Constitution, and laws of the United States, shall be extended, and govern the said courts in the trial and disposition of such causes, and, if of a criminal nature, in the infliction of punishment on the party found guilty.

§ 4. That the district attorneys, marshals, and deputy marshals, of the United States, the commissioners appointed by the circuit and territorial courts of the United States, with power of arresting, imprisoning, or bailing offenders against the laws of the United States, the officers and agents of the Freedmen's Bureau, and every other officer who may be specially empowered by the President of the United States, shall be, and they are, hereby specially authorized and required, at the expense of the United States, to institute proceedings against all and every person who shall violate the provisions of this act, and cause him or them to be arrested and imprisoned, or bailed, as the case may be, for trial before such of the United States or territorial courts as by this act have cognizance of the offence, and, with a view to affording reasonable protection to all persons in their constitutional rights of equality before the law, without distinction of race or color, or previous condition of slavery or involuntary servitude, except as a punishment for crime, whereof the party shall have been duly convicted, and the prompt discharge of the duties of this act, it shall be the duty of the circuit courts of the United States and the superior courts of the territories of the United States, from time to time, to increase the number of Commissioners, so as to afford a speedy and convenient means for the arrest and examination of persons charged with a violation of this act.

§ 5. That said Commissioners shall have concurrent jurisdiction with the judges of the circuit and district courts of the United States, and the judges of the superior courts of the territories, severally and collectively, in term time and vacation, upon satisfactory proof being made, to issue warrants and precepts for arresting and bringing before them all offenders against the provisions of this act, and, on examination, to discharge, admit to bail, or commit them for trial, as the facts may warrant.

§ 6. And such Commissioners are hereby authorized and required to exercise and discharge all the powers and duties conferred on them by this Act, and the same duties with regard to offences created by this act, as they are authorized by law to exercise with regard to other offences against the laws of the United States. That it shall be the duty of all marshals and deputy marshals to obey and execute all warrants and precepts issued under the provisions of this act when to them directed, and should any marshal or deputy marshal refuse to receive such warrant or other process, when tendered, or to use all proper means diligently to execute the same, he shall on conviction thereof be fined in the sum of one thousand dollars, to the use of the person upon whom the accused is alleged to have committed the offence; and the better to enable the said Commissioners to execute their duties faithfully and efficiently, in conformity with the Constitution of the United States, and the requirements of this act, they are hereby authorized and empowered, within their counties respectively, to appoint, in writing under their hands, one or more suitable persons, from time to time, to execute all such warrants and other process as may be issued by them in the lawful performance of their respective duties, and the person so appointed to execute any warrant or process as aforesaid shall have authority to summon and call to their aid the bystanders of a *posse comitatus* of the proper county, or such portion of the land or naval forces of the United States, or of the militia, as may be necessary to the performance of the duty with which they are charged, and to insure a faithful observance of the clause of the Constitution which prohibits slavery, in conformity with the provisions of this act; and said warrants shall run and be executed by said officers anywhere in the State or Territory within which they are issued.

§ 7. That any person who shall knowingly and wrongfully obstruct, hinder or prevent any officer or other person charged with the execution of any warrant or process issued under the provisions of this act, or any person or persons lawfully assisting him or them, from arresting any person for whose apprehension such warrant or process may have been issued; or shall rescue, or attempt to rescue, such person from the custody of the officer, other person or persons, or those lawfully assisting, as aforesaid, when so arrested, pursuant to the authority herein given and declared; or shall aid, abet or assist any person so arrested as aforesaid, directly or indirectly, to escape from the custody of the officer or other persons legally authorized, as aforesaid, or shall harbor or conceal any person for whom a warrant or process shall have been issued as aforesaid, so as to prevent his discovery and arrest after notice of knowledge of the fact that a warrant has been issued for the apprehension of such person, shall for either of said offences be subject to a fine not exceeding one thousand dollars, and imprisonment not exceeding six months, by indictment before the district court of the United States for the district in which said offence may have been committed, or before the proper court of criminal jurisdiction, if committed within any one of the organized Territories of the United States.

§ 8. That the district attorneys, the marshals, their deputies, and the clerks of the said district and territorial courts, shall be paid for their services the like fees as may be allowed to them for similar services in other cases; and in all cases where the proceedings are before a Commissioner he shall be entitled to a fee of ten dollars in full for his services in each case, inclusive of all services incident to such arrest and examination. The person or persons authorized to execute the process to be issued by such Commissioners for the arrest of offenders against the provisions of this act, shall be entitled to a fee of five dollars for each person he or they may arrest and take before any such Commissioner, as aforesaid, with such other fees as may be deemed reasonable by such Commissioner for such other additional services as may be necessarily performed by him or them—such as attending at the examination, keeping the prisoner in custody, and providing food and lodgings during his detention and until the final determination of such Commissioner, and in general for performing such other duties as may be required in the premises, such fees to be made up in conformity with the fees usually charged by the officers of the court of justice, within the proper district or county, as near as practicable, and paid out of the Treasury of the United States, on the certificate of the district within which the arrest is made, and to be recoverable from the defendant as part of the judgment in case of conviction.

§ 9. That whenever the President of the United States shall have reason to believe that offences have been or are likely to be committed against the provisions of this act within any judicial district, it shall be lawful for him, in his discretion, to direct the judge, marshal and district attorney of such district to attend at such place within the district and for such time as he may designate, for the purpose of the more speedy arrest and trial of persons charged with the violation of this act; and it shall be the duty of every judge or other officer, when any such requisition shall be received by him, to attend at the place and for the time therein designated.

§ 10. That it shall be lawful for the President of the United States, or such persons as he may empower for that purpose, to employ such part of the land or naval forces of the United States, or of the militia, as shall be necessary to prevent the violation and enforce the due execution of this act.

§ 11. That upon all questions of law arising in any cause under the provisions of this act, a final appeal may be taken to the supreme court of the United States.

FREEDMEN'S BUREAU BILL,

AS AMENDED AND APPROVED BY THE XXXIXTH CONGRESS.

AN ACT to continue in force and to amend "An act to establish a Bureau for the Relief of Freedmen and Refugees," and for other purposes.

Be it enacted by the Senate and House of Representatives of the United States of America in Congress assembled, That the act to establish a Bureau for the Relief of Freedmen and Refugees, approved March third, eighteen hundred and sixty-five, shall continue in force for the term of two years from and after the passage of this act.

§ 2. *And be it further enacted*, That the supervision and care of said bureau shall extend to all loyal refugees and freedmen, so far as the same shall be necessary to enable them as speedily as practicable to become self-supporting citizens of the United States, and to aid them in making the freedom conferred by proclamation of the commander-in-chief, by emancipation under the laws of States, and by constitutional amendment, available to them and beneficial to the republic.

§ 3. *And be it further enacted*, That the President shall, by and with the advice and consent of the Senate, appoint two assistant commissioners in addition to those authorized by the act to which this is an amendment, who shall give like bonds and receive the same annual salary provided in said act, and each of the assistant commissioners of the bureau shall have charge of one district containing such refugees or freedmen, to be assigned him by the Commissioner, with the approval of the President. And the Commissioner shall, under the direction of the President, and so far as the same shall be, in his judgment, necessary for the efficient and economical administration of the affairs of the bureau, appoint such agents, clerks, and assistants as may be required for the proper conduct of the bureau. Military officers or enlisted men may be detailed for service and assigned to duty under this act; and the President may, if in his judgment safe and judicious so to do, detail from the army all the officers and agents of this bureau; but no officer so assigned shall have increase of pay or allowances. Each agent or clerk, not heretofore authorized by law, not being a military officer, shall have an annual salary of not less than five hundred dollars, nor more than twelve hundred dollars, according to the service required of him. And it shall be the duty of the Commissioner, when it can be done consistently with public interest, to appoint, as assistant commissioners, agents, and clerks, such men as have proved their loyalty by faithful service in the armies of the Union during the rebellion. And all persons appointed to service under this act and the act to which this is an amendment shall be so far deemed in the military service of the United States as to be under the military jurisdiction, and entitled to the military protection of the government while in discharge of the duties of their office.

§ 4. *And be it further enacted*, That officers of the Veteran Reserve Corps or of the volunteer service, now on duty in the Freedmen's Bureau as assistant commissioners, agents, medical officers, or in other capacities, whose regiments or corps have been or may hereafter be mustered out of service, may be retained upon such duty as officers of said bureau, with the same compensation as is now provided by law for their respective grades; and the Secretary of War shall have power to fill vacancies until other officers can be detailed in their places without detriment to the public service.

§ 5. *And be it further enacted*, That the second section of the act to which this is an amendment shall be deemed to authorize the Secretary of War to issue such medical stores or other supplies and transportation, and afford such medical or other aid as may be needful for the purpose named in said section: *Provided*, That no person shall be deemed "destitute," "suffering," or "dependent upon the government for support," within the meaning of this act, who is able to find employment, and could, by proper industry and exertion, avoid such destitution, suffering, or dependence.

§ 6. Whereas, by the provisions of an act approved February sixth, eighteen hundred and sixty-three, entitled "An act to amend an act entitled 'An act for the collection of direct taxes in insurrectionary districts within the United States, and for other purposes,' approved June seventh, eighteen hundred and sixty-two," certain lands in the parishes of Saint Helena and Saint Luke, South Carolina, were bid in by the United States at public tax sales, and by the limitation of said act the time of redemption of said lands has expired; and whereas, in accordance with instructions issued by President Lincoln on the sixteenth day of September, eighteen hundred and sixty-three, to the United States direct tax commissioners for South Carolina, certain lands bid in by the United States in the parish of Saint Helena, in said State, were in part sold by the said tax commissioners to "heads of families of the African race," in parcels of not more than twenty acres to each purchaser; and whereas, under the said instructions, the said tax commissioners did also set apart as "school farms" certain parcels of land in said parish, numbered on their plats from one to thirty-three, inclusive, making an aggregate of six thousand acres, more or less: *Therefore, be it further enacted*, That the sales made to "heads of families of the African race," under the instructions of President Lincoln to the United States direct tax commissioners for South Carolina, of date of September sixteenth, eighteen hundred and sixty-three, are hereby confirmed and established; and all leases which have been made to such "heads of families," by said direct tax commissioners, shall be changed into certificates of sale in all cases wherein the lease provides for such substitution; and all the lands now remaing unsold, which come within the same designation, being eight thousand acres, more or less, shall be disposed of according to said instructions.

§ 7. *And be it further enacted*, That all other lands bid in by the United States at tax sales, being thirty-eight thousand acres, more or less, and now in the hands of the said tax commissioners as the property of the United States, in the parishes of Saint Helena and Saint Luke, excepting the "school farms," as specified in the preceding section, and so much as may be necessary for military and naval purposes at Hilton Head, Bay Point, and Land's End, and excepting also the city of Port Royal, on Saint Helena island, and the town of Beaufort, shall be disposed of in parcels of twenty acres, at one dollar and fifty cents per acre, to such persons, and to such only, as have acquired and are now occupying lands under and agreeably to the provisions of General Sherman's special field order, dated at Savannah, Georgia, January sixteenth, eighteen hundred and sixty-five, and the remaining lands, if any, shall be disposed of in like manner to such persons as had acquired lands agreeably to the said order of General Sherman, but who have been dispossessed by the restoration of the same to former owners: *Provided*, That the lands sold in compliance with the provisions of this and the preceding section shall not be alienated by their purchasers within six years from and after the passage of this act.

§ 8. *And be it further enacted*, That the "school farms" in the parish of Saint Helena, South Carolina, shall be sold, subject to any leases of the same, by the said tax commissioners, at public auction, on or before the first day of January, eighteen hundred and sixty-seven, at not less than ten dollars per acre; and the lots in the city of Port Royal, as laid down by the said tax commissioners, and the lots and houses in the town of Beaufort, which are still held in like manner, shall be sold at public auction; and the proceeds of said sales, after paying expenses of the surveys and sales, shall be invested in United States bonds, the interest of which shall be appropriated, under the direction of the Commissioner, to the support of schools, without distinction of color or race, on the islands in the parishes of Saint Helena and Saint Luke.

§ 9. *And be it further enacted*, That the assistant commissioners for South Carolina and Georgia are hereby authorized to examine all claims to lands in their respective States which are claimed under the provisions of General Sherman's special field order, and to give each person having a valid claim a warrant upon the direct tax commissioners for South Carolina for twenty acres of land, and the said direct tax commissioners shall issue to every person, or to his or her heirs, but in no case to any assigns, presenting such warrant, a lease of twenty acres of land, as provided for in section 7, for the term of six years; but at any time thereafter, upon the payment of a sum not exceeding one dollar and fifty cents per acre, the person holding such lease shall be entitled to a certificate of sale of said tract of twenty acres from the direct tax commissioner or such officer as may be authorized to issue the same; but no warrant shall be held valid longer than two years after the issue of the same.

§ 10. *And be it further enacted*, That the direct tax commissioners for South Carolina are hereby authorized and required at the earliest day practicable to survey the lands designated in section 7 into lots of twenty acres each, with proper metes and bounds distinctly marked, so that the several tracts shall be convenient in form, and as near as practicable have an average of fertility and woodland; and the expense of such surveys shall be paid from the proceeds of the sales of said lands, or, if sooner required, out of any moneys received for other lands on these islands, sold by the United States for taxes, and now in the hands of the direct tax commissioners.

§ 11. *And be it further enacted*, That restoration of lands occupied by freedmen under General Sherman's field order, dated at Savannah, Georgia, January sixteenth, eighteen hundred and sixty-five, shall not be made until after the crops of the present year shall have been gathered by the occupants of said lands, nor until a fair compensation shall have been made to them by the former owners of such lands or their legal representatives for all improvements or betterments erected or constructed thereon, and after due notice of the same being done shall have been given by the assistant commissioner.

§ 12. *And be it further enacted*, That the Commissioner shall have power to seize, hold, use, lease, or sell all buildings and tenements, and any lands appertaining to the same, or otherwise, formerly held under color of title by the late so-called Confederate States, and not heretofore disposed of by the United States, and any buildings or lands held in trust for the same by any person or persons, and to use the same or appropriate the proceeds derived therefrom to the education of the freed people; and whenever the bureau shall cease to exist, such of said so-called Confederate States as shall have made provision for the education of their citizens without distinction of color shali receive the sum remaining unexpended of such sales or rentals, which shall be distributed among said States for educational purposes in proportion to their population.

§ 13. *And be it further enacted*, That the Commissioner of this bureau shall at all times co-operate with private benevolent associations of citizens in aid of freedmen, and with agents and teachers, duly accredited and appointed by them, and shall hire or provide by lease buildings for purposes of education whenever such associations shall, without cost to the government, provide suitable teachers and means of instructions; and he shall furnish such protection as may be required for the safe conduct of such schools.

§ 14. *And be it further enacted*, That in every State or district where the ordinary course of judicial proceedings has been interrupted by the rebellion, and until the same shall be fully restored, and in every State or district whose constitutional relations to the government have been practically discontinued by the rebellion, and until such State shall have been restored in such relations, and shall be duly represented in the Congress of the United States, the right to make and enforce contracts, to sue, be parties, and give evidence, to inherit, purchase, lease, sell, hold, and convey real and personal property, and to have full and equal benefit of all laws and proceedings concerning personal liberty, personal security, and the acquisition, enjoyment, and disposition of estate, real and personal, including the constitutional right to bear arms, shall be secured to and enjoyed by all the citizens of such State or district without respect to race or color, or previous condition of slavery. And whenever in either of said States or districts the ordinary course of judicial proceedings has been interrupted by the rebellion, and until the same shall be fully restored, and until such State shall have been restored in its constitutional relations to the government, and shall be duly represented in the Congress of the United States, the President shall, through the Commissioner and the officers of the bureau, and under such rules and regulations as the President, through the Secretary of War, shall prescribe, extend military protection and have military jurisdiction over all cases and questions concerning the free enjoyment of such immunities and rights, and no penalty or punishment for any violation of law shall be imposed or permitted because of race or color, or previous condition of slavery, other or greater than the penalty or punishment to which white persons may be liable by law for the like offence. But the jurisdiction conferred by this section upon the officers of the bureau shall not exist in any State where the ordinary course of judicial proceedings has not been interrupted by the rebellion, and shall cease in every State when the courts of the State and of the United States are not disturbed in the peaceable course of justice, and after such State shall be fully restored in its constitutional relations to the government, and shall be duly represented in the Congress of the United States.

§ 15. *And be it further enacted*, That all officers, agents, and employés of this bureau, before entering upon the duties of their office, shall take the oath prescribed in the first section of the act to which this is an amendment; and all acts or parts of acts inconsistent with the provisions of this act are hereby repealed.

SCHUYLER COLFAX,
Speaker of the House of Representatives.
LAFAYETTE S. FOSTER,
President of Senate pro tempore.

IN THE HOUSE OF REPRESENTATIVES UNITED STATES,
July 16, 1866.

The President of the United States having returned to the House of Representatives, in which it originated, the bill entitled "An act to continue in force and to amend 'An act to establish a Bureau for the Relief of Freedmen and Refugees,' and for other purposes," with his objections thereto, the House of Representatives proceeded, in pursuance of the Constitution to reconsider the same; and

Resolved, That the said bill pass, two-thirds of the House of Representatives agreeing to pass the same.

Attest: EDWARD MCPHERSON,
Clerk House of Representatives of the United States.

IN SENATE OF THE UNITED STATES,
July 16, 1866.

The Senate having proceeded, in pursuance of the Constitution, to reconsider the bill entitled "An act to continue in force and to amend 'An act to establish a Bureau for the Relief of Freedmen and Refugess,' and for other purposes," returned to the House of Representatives by the President of the United States, with his objections, and sent by the House of Representatives to the Senate with the message of the President returning the bill—

Resolved, That the bill do pass, two-thirds of the Senate agreeing to pass the same.

Attest: J. W. FORNEY,
Secretary of the Senate of the United States.

PROVOST MARSHAL-GENERAL'S REPORT.

SHOWING THE NUMBER OF MEN ENLISTED, NUMBER OF KILLED, WOUNDED, AND DEATHS FROM DISEASE, DURING THE REBELLION.

WASHINGTON, D. C., Friday, April 27, 1866.

THE following is a condensed summary of the results of the operations of this bureau, from its organization to the close of the war.

1. By means of a full and exact enrollment of all persons liable to conscription, under the law of March 3 and its amendments, a complete exhibit of the military resources of the loyal States, in men, was made, showing an aggregate number of 2,254,063, not including 1,000,516 soldiers actually under arms, when hostilities ceased.

2. One million one hundred and twenty thousand six hundred and twenty-one men were raised, at an average cost (on account of recruitment exclusive of

bounties,) of $9.84 per man, while the cost of recruiting of 1,356,593 raised prior to the organization of the Bureau was $34.01 per man. A saving of over seventy cents on the dollar in the cost of raising troops was thus effected under this Bureau, notwithstanding the increase in the price of subsistence, transportation, rents, &c., during the last two years of the war. (Item: The number above given does not embrace the naval credits allowed under the eighth section of the act of July 4, 1864, nor credits for drafted men who paid commutation, the recruits for the regular army, nor the credits allowed by the Adjutant-General subsequent to May 25, 1865, for men raised prior to that date.)

3. Seventy-six thousand five hundred and twenty-six deserters were arrested and returned to the army. The vigilance and energy of the officers of the Bureau, in this line of the business, put an effectual check to the wide-spread evil of desertion, which, at one time, impaired so seriously the numerical strength and efficiency of the army.

4. The quotas of men furnished by the various parts of the country were equalized, and a proportionate share of military service secured from each, thus removing the very serious inequality of recruitment, which had arisen during the first two years of the war, and which, when the bureau was organized,

had become an almost insuperable obstacle to the further progress of raising troops.

5. Records were completed showing minutely the physical condition of 1,014,776 of the men examined, and tables of great scientific and professional value have been compiled from this data.

6. The casualties in the entire military force of the nation during the war of the rebellion, as shown by the official muster-rolls and monthly returns, have been compiled with, in part, this result:

KILLED IN ACTION OR DIED OF WOUNDS WHILE IN SERVICE.	
Commissioned officers	5,221
Enlisted men	90,868
DIED FROM DISEASE OR ACCIDENT.	
Commissioned officers	2,321
Enlisted men	182,329
Total loss in service	280,739

These figures have been carefully compiled from the complete official file of muster-rolls and monthly returns, but yet entire accuracy is not claimed for them, as errors and omissions to some extent doubtless prevailed in the rolls and returns. Deaths (from wounds or disease contracted in service) which occurred after the men left the army are not included in these figures.

7. The system of recruitment established by the Bureau, under the laws of Congress, if permanently adopted, (with such improvement as experience may suggest,) will be capable of maintaining the numerical strength and improving the character of the army in time of peace, or of promptly and economically rendering available the National forces to any required extent in time of war.

THE UNITED STATES ARMY DURING THE GREAT CIVIL WAR OF 1861-65.

THE following statement shows the number of men furnished by each State:

STATES.	Men furnished under Act of April 15, 1861, for 75,000 militia for 3 months.	Aggregate No. of men furnish'd under all calls.	Aggregate No. of men furnish'd under all calls, reduced to the 3 years' standard.
Maine	771	71.745	56,595
New Hampshire	779	34,605	30,827
Vermont	782	35,246	29,052
Massachusetts	3,736	151,785	123,844
Rhode Island	3,147	23,711	17,878
Connecticut	2,402	57,270	50,514
New York	13,906	464,156	381,696
New Jersey	3,123	79,511	55,785
Pennsylvania	20,175	366,326	267,558
Delaware	775	13,651	10,303
Maryland	......	49,731	40,692
West Virginia	900	32,003	27,653
District of Columbia	4,720	16,872	11,506
Ohio	12,357	317,133	237,976
Indiana	4,686	195,147	152,283
Illinois	4,820	258,217	212,694
Michigan	781	90,119	80,865
Wisconson	817	96,118	78,985
Minnesota	930	25,034	19,675
Iowa	968	75,860	68,182
Missouri	10,501	108,773	86,192
Kentucky	......	78,540	70,348
Kansas	650	20,097	18,654
Tennessee	......	12,077	12,077
Arkansas	......	......	......
North Carolina	......	......	......
California	......	7,451	7,451
Nevada	......	216	216
Oregon	......	617	581
Washington Ter'ty.	......	895	895
Nebraska	......	1,279	380
Colorado	......	1,762	1,762
Dakota	......	181	181
New Mexico	1,510	2,395	1,011
Total	93,326	2,688,523	2,154,311

HISTORY OF THE FLAG.

BY A DISTINGUISHED HISTORIAN.

Men, in the aggregate, demand something besides abstract ideas and principles. Hence the desire for symbols—something visible to the eye and that appeals to the senses. Every nation has a flag that represents the country—every army a common banner, which, to the soldier, stands for that army. It speaks to him in the din of battle, cheers him in the long and tedious march, and pleads with him on the disastrous retreat.

Standards were originally carried on a pole or lance. It matters little what they may be, for the symbol is the same.

In ancient times the Hebrew tribes had each its own standard—that of Ephraim, for instance, was a steer; of Benjamin, a wolf. Among the Greeks, the Athenians had an owl, and the Thebans a sphynx. The standard of Romulus was a bundle of hay tied to a pole, afterwards a human hand, and finally an eagle.

Eagles were at first made of wood, then of silver, with thunderbolts of gold. Under Cæsar they were all gold, without thunderbolts, and were carried on a long pike. The Germans formerly fastened a streamer to a lance, which the duke carried in front of the army. Russia and Austria adopted the double headed eagle. The ancient national flag of England, all know, was the banner of St. George, a white field with a red cross. This was at first used in the Colonies, but several changes were afterwards made.

Of course, when they separated from the mother country, it was necessary to have a distinct flag of their own, and the Continental Congress appointed Dr. Franklin, Mr. Lynch, and Mr. Harrison, a committee to take the subject into consideration. They repaired to the American army, a little over 9,000 strong, then assembled at Cambridge, and after due consideration, adopted one composed of seven white and seven red stripes, with the red and white crosses of St. George and St. Andrew, conjoined on a blue field in the corner, and named it "The Great Union Flag." The crosses of St. George and St. Andrew were retained to show the willingness of the colonies to return to their allegiance to the British crown, if their rights were secured. This flag was first hoisted on the first day of January, 1776. In the meantime, the various colonies had adopted distinctive badges, so that the different bodies of troops, that flocked to the army, had each its own banner. In Connecticut, each regiment had its own peculiar standard, on which were represented the arms of the colony, with the motto, "Qui transtulit sustinet"—(he who transplanted us will sustain us.) The one that Putnam gave to the breeze on Prospect Hill on the 18th of July, 1775, was a red flag, with this motto on one side, and on the other, the words inscribed, "An appeal to Heaven." That of the floating batteries was a white ground with the same "Appeal to Heaven" upon it. It is supposed that at Bunker Hill our troops carried a red flag, with a pine tree on a white field in the corner. The first flag in South Carolina was blue, with a crescent in the corner, and received its first baptism under Moultrie. In 1776, Col. Gadsen presented to Congress a flag to be used by the navy, which consisted of a rattle-snake on a yellow ground, with thirteen rattles, and coiled to strike. The motto was, "Don't tread on me." "The Great Union Flag," as described above, without the crosses, and sometimes with the rattle-snake and motto, "Don't tread on me," was used as a naval flag, and called the "Continental Flag."

As the war progressed, different regiments and corps adopted peculiar flags, by which they were designated. The troops which Patrick Henry raised and called the "Culpepper Minute Men," had a banner with a rattle-snake on it, and the mottoes, "Don't tread on me," and "Liberty or death," together with their name. Morgan's celebrated riflemen, called the "Morgan Rifles," not only had a peculiar uniform, but a flag of their own, on which was inscribed, "XI. Virginia Regiment," and the words, "Morgan's Rifle Corps." On it was also the date, 1776, surrounded by a wreath of laurel. Wherever this banner floated, the soldiers knew that deadly work was being done.

When the gallant Pulaski was raising a body of cavalry, in Baltimore, the nuns of Bethlehem sent him a banner of crimson silk, with emblems on it, wrought by their own hands. That of Washington's Life Guard was made of white silk, with various devices upon it, and the motto, "Conquer or die."

It doubtless always will be customary in this country, during a war, for different regiments to have flags presented to them with various devices upon them. It was so during the recent war, but as the stars and stripes supplant them all, so in our revolutionary struggle, the "Great Union Flag," which was raised in Cambridge, took the place of all others and became the flag of the American army.

But in 1777, Congress, on the 19th day of June, passed the following resolution: "*Resolved*, That the flag of the thirteen United States be thirteen stripes, alternate red and white, that the union be thirteen stars, white, in a blue field, representing a new constellation." A constellation, however, could not well be represented on a flag, and so it was changed into a circle of stars, to represent harmony and union. Red is supposed to represent courage, white, integrity of purpose, and blue, steadfastness, love, and faith. This flag, however, was not used till the following autumn, and waved first over the memorable battle field of Saratoga.

Thus our flag was born, which to-day is known, respected, and feared round the entire globe. In 1794 it received a slight modification, evidently growing out of the intention at that time of Congress to add a new stripe with every additional State that came into the Union, for it passed that year the following resolution: "*Resolved*, That from and after the 1st day of May, Anno Domini 1795, the flag of the United States be fifteen stripes, alternate red and white. That the union be fifteen stars, white, in a blue field." In 1818, it was by another resolution of Congress, changed back into thirteen stripes, with twenty-one stars, in which it was provided that a new star should be added to the union on the admission of each new State. That resolution has never been rescinded, till now thirty-six stars blaze on our banner. The symbol of our nationality, the record of our glory, it has become dear to the heart of the people. On the sea and on the land its history has been one to swell the heart with pride. The most beautiful flag in the world in its appearance, it is stained by no disgrace, for it has triumphed in every struggle. Through three wars it bore us on to victory, and in this last terrible struggle against treason, though baptized in the blood of its own children, not a star has been effaced, and it still waves over a united nation.

Whenever the "Star-Spangled Banner" is sung, the spontaneous outburst of the vast masses, as the chorus is reached, shows what a hold that flag has on the popular heart. It not only represents our nationality, but it is the *people's* flag. It led them on to freedom—it does something more than appeal to their pride as a symbol of national greatness—it appeals to their affections as a friend of their dearest rights. We cannot better close this short history of our flag than by appending the following stirring poem of Drake:

WHEN freedom from her mountain height
  Unfurled her standard to the air,
She tore the azure robes of night,
  And set the stars of glory there!

She mingled with its gorgeous dyes
The milky baldric of the skies,
And striped its pure celestial white
With streakings of the morning light;
Then, from his mansion in the sun,
She called her eagle-bearer down,
And gave into his mighty hand
The symbol of her chosen land!

Majestic monarch of the cloud
   Who rear'st aloft thy regal form,
To hear the tempest trumping loud
And see the lightning lances driven,
   When strive the warriors of the storm,
And rolls the thunder drum of heaven,
Child of the sun! to thee 'tis given
   To guard the banner of the free;
To hover in the sulphur smoke,
To ward away the battle stroke;
And bid its blendings shine afar,
Like rainbows on the cloud of war—
   The harbinger of victory!

Flag of the brave! thy folds shall fly,
The sign of hope and triumph high,
When speaks the signal trumpet tone,
And the long line comes gleaming on,
(Ere yet the life-blood, warm and wet,
Hath dimmed the glittering bayonet,)
Each soldier's eye shall brightly turn
To where thy sky-born giories burn,

And, as his springing steps advance,
Catch war and vengeance from the glance;
And when the cannon's mouthings loud
Heave in wild wreaths the battle shroud,
And gory sabres rise and fall,
Like shoots of flame on midnight's pall;
Then shall thy meteor glances glow,
　And cowering foes shall shrink beneath
Each gallant arm that strikes below
　That lovely messenger of death.

Flag of the seas! on ocean wave
Thy stars shall glitter o'er the brave,
When death, careering on the gale,
Sweeps darkly round the bellied sail,
And frightened waves rush wildly back,
Before the broadside's reeling rack,
Each dying wanderer of the sea,
Shall look at once to heaven and thee,
And smile to see thy splendor fly,
In triumph o'er his closing eye.

Flag of the free, heart's hope and home!
　By angel hands to valor given;
Thy stars have lit the welkin dome,
　And all thy hues were born in heaven!
Forever float that standard sheet!
　Where breathes the foe but falls before us?
With Freedom's soil beneath our feet,
　And Freedom's banner streaming o'er us?

www.ingramcontent.com/pod-product-compliance
Lightning Source LLC
LaVergne TN
LVHW010234110826
845151LV00004B/1293

* 9 7 8 1 4 2 5 5 2 5 0 6 4 *